IRISH EMIGRATION

TO THE

UNITED STATES:

WHAT IT HAS BEEN, AND WHAT IT IS.

Facts and Reflections especially addressed to Irish People intending to emigrate from their native land; and to those living in the large cities of Great Britain and of the United States.

BY

THE REV. STEPHEN BYRNE, O.S.D.

NEW YORK:
THE CATHOLIC PUBLICATION SOCIETY,
No. 9 WARREN STREET.

1873.

Approbatio Ordinis.

IMPRIMATUR.

FR. VINCENTIUS HIGGINS, O.P.,
FR. ANTONINUS SPENCER, O.P.,
Revisores Ordinis.

JOHN ROSS & CO., PRINTERS, 27 ROSE STREET, NEW YORK.

PREFACE.

IN preparing this work for the perusal of Irish emigrants and their children, there is not the least intention of encouraging more emigration, especially from Ireland, than has already taken place. But inasmuch as it still goes on, and is likely to continue for years to come, the information and suggestions contained herein may be useful to many—hurtful to none. I must acknowledge, in fact, that the real motive of putting these pages into print is the following: A large number of emigrants from Ireland, in leaving their homes either from choice or necessity, have made, I think, a very fatal mistake in crowding into the large cities of England, Scotland, and America. By all who have given the subject any consideration, as well as by those who have made it a study, the conclusion has been reached that it would have been far better for the majority of them to have sought employment and homes on the vacant or semi-vacant lands of the United States. It is highly probable that many among them are prepared to rectify the mistake, if they only know where to go. The object, therefore, of this publication is to supply that information as far as it can be done in a brief space.

The work is in two parts: the *first* contains information and directions of a general character respecting the prospects, duties, dangers, and mistakes of emigrants; the *second part* contains as exact a statement, probably, as can be found of the population, area, and general resources of each State and Territory, based upon the United States Census Report for 1870. Appended to the account of each State and Territory, in the material point of view, is an account of the condition of the Catholic Church in each, based upon the statistics given in the *Catholic*

Almanac of 1873, or taken from letters actually received from the Most Rev. and Right Rev. Archbishops and Bishops of the country, nearly all of whom were applied to for information.

In preparing the work, I wrote also to about thirty Governors of States and Territories for special information regarding their respective localities. Answers and pamphlets have been received from nearly all of them, which are made use of extensively in the *second part* of the work.

At first it was intended to have published a larger work; but reflection on the subject dictated the greater utility of a short treatise which would not be too dear to be bought, or too diffuse to be read, by those for whom it is intended. It may not be amiss to say that the work, such as it is, is the result of more than twenty years' actual observation of immigrant life in most of the States and in many of the large cities of the Union. If only one thousand persons are benefited by the perusal of these pages, or if any are rescued from the evil influences and wretched poverty of immigrant life in large cities, the writer will have received his reward.

AUGUST 4, 1873.

CONTENTS.

PART FIRST.

CHAPTER I.

CHAPTER II.

CHAPTER III.

CHAPTER IV.

CHAPTER V.

CHAPTER VI.

CHAPTER VII.

PART SECOND.

CHAPTER VII.

CHAPTER VIII.

CHAPTER IX.

CHAPTER X.

TABLE I.

TABLE II.—FARM LABOR.

TABLE III.—MECHANICAL LABOR.

TABLE IV.

TABLE V.

IRISH EMIGRATION

TO THE

UNITED STATES.

CHAPTER I.

GENERAL VIEW OF THE SUBJECT.

FROM the statistics of immigration into the United States, it appears evident that the influx from Ireland is by no means exhausted. Thus we see that in the year 1872, the emigration from that island reached the important figure of 68,745 souls. During the fifty-two years beginning with the year 1820, when exact statistics of the numbers and nationality of immigrants began to be kept, it is proved beyond question that the total number of the natives of Ireland who have sought homes in the United States may be set down as four millions of souls. And it is highly probable that the number coming directly from Ireland, and those Irish people who emigrate from British cities, will, in the next ten years, make up another million. Much of the unprecedented development and prosperity of the United States is due to the hardy energy and remarkable perseverance of our race. But it may be well to put ourselves the question: Have we as a people paid sufficient attention to the proper establishing of ourselves in a state, not merely of prosperity, but of simple competency or independence in this great country? Let the crowded tenement-houses of Eastern cities, where the very atmosphere is poisoned by the occupancy in one house of from twenty to forty families, and where morality itself is greatly endangered on account of associations that cannot be avoided, answer. Let the unnamed and unnumbered graves along the canals and railroads of the United States, answer. Let the forlorn and forgotten creatures who, having neither homes nor friends, lie down and die in the common hospitals of the country, answer. The response comes home to us in a hundred forms that, *as a people*, we have, whilst doing more than any other to build up this great Republic, been rather negligent, not to say reckless, in regard to our individual interests. I have not time to develop in detail the causes of this indifference; but whoever reads carefully the history of our island from 1692 to 1829—the period pre-eminently of the penal laws—will at once conclude that a people so crushed, so bewildered, so robbed, not only of their lands, but also of nearly every species of human industry, excepting agriculture,—will honestly conclude that, if many of the immigrants from Ireland to America of the last fifty years were wanting in some of the qualities that make nations and individuals prosperous, it is not wonderful. I will glance at another cause. The love we bear to our native land is, next after our faith, a love of peculiar intensity. We all dream of a free, a happy, and a prosperous Ireland. No true man of any race or nation will condemn this sentiment. The retrospective view of Ireland, of her wrongs and sufferings, sometimes interferes, however, with the present and prospective view of our opportunities and duties in the land of our adoption. The direct object of these pages is to awaken thought as to the best means of remedying this evil.

In the *first place*, it is well to reflect that, in the providence of the great God, we inhabit here a vast continent. It is the great domain that he offers to the oppressed and industrious poor of all nations under heaven. The immigrants of the past and of the present are made partakers of its freedom, its hospitality; of the opportunities it affords to all who will enjoy them of making for themselves and children independent homes. To-day we number about forty millions in the United States. In the year 1800, the population was only five millions and one half, and in 1820, only ten millions. The year 1900 will, in all human probability, open upon one hundred millions of human beings inhabiting what is now known as the United States of North America. Taking the whole country into account, therefore, and its grand future, the immigrants of the last twenty-five years and of the present time, it may be truly said, are first in this vast field of human enterprise. Being first in the field, it would be foolish not to turn our advantages to account.

Secondly. The dream of a free and a happy Ireland is most excusable, not to say commendable. But however free and happy Ireland may be, very few of her millions of children now living in America, and fewer still of *their* children, will make of it the home of their old age. Therefore, even if we regard our separation from our native land as a species of exile, still we must look upon it as a settled fact, and, as men of common sense, make the best of it.

Thirdly. To all who can have no hope of obtaining independent homes in large cities, I would say, reflect deeply upon this important subject. In a country so young, a country where land is so cheap, all of its inhabitants ought to have their own homes. The great West invites the people of the world to its broad prairies and grand forests; the South also is now open to the enterprise of *white labor*, and the leading men of that section are fully alive to the importance of immigration, and are leaving nothing undone by which they can hope to promote the settlement of Europeans in that part of the country.

CHAPTER II.

IRISH EMIGRATION IN THE PAST—ITS VALUE TO THE UNITED STATES.

BEFORE the year 1820, no official statistics of immigration into the United States were kept. There are no certain means, therefore, by which we may come to anything like an exact calculation of the numbers arriving before that time. But there are means in abundance by which to judge the special locations of the different nationalities before the Revolution and since. Thus we find that, while Maryland and Pennsylvania were the principal receptacles of Irish immigration before the year 1800, great numbers also found their way into New Hampshire, Virginia (especially into the valley of the Shenandoah), and into North and South Carolina.

The War of Independence commenced with the battle of Lexington, near Boston, on the 19th of April, 1775, and ended with the treaty of peace in February, 1783. Through these eight eventful years, we find a very large proportion of Celtic names on the military, naval, and civil lists of each of the thirteen United Colonies. They are especially prominent in Pennsylvania, where we find five Irish colonels at the head of as many regiments, principally made up of soldiers of the same nationality. This was the celebrated Pennsylvania line, so well known in Revolutionary history. We also find them in large numbers in the Maryland line, and among the volunteers generally. John Barry, who is called the father of the American navy, and a large number of the other naval officers of that period, were Irish by birth or immediate descent. The grand charter of American liberty—the Declaration of Independence—was signed on the 4th of July, 1776, by fifty-six delegates, representing the thirteen original States; of this number, nine were of the Irish race. They filled many civil positions of great trust and responsibility in those early days of the American Republic. This is not mentioned in any spirit of boastfulness, but merely to show that there was a respectable number of the race in America before the Revolution. Thus it is that the Hon. Edward Young, Chief of the Bureau of Statistics in Washington, in his very able Report on the Statistics of Immigration, published in connection with the census report of 1870, says: "The population of the Colonies at the beginning of the Revolutionary War has generally been estimated at three millions; and it is probable that as many as one-third of these were born on the other side of the Atlantic, while the parents of a large proportion of the remainder were among the early immigrants." What proportion of these were Irish we may judge from the fact that, in the year 1729, of the total number of immigrant passengers (6,500) arriving at the port of Philadelphia alone, 5,600 were Irish.

Immigration was in a great degree suspended during the War of Independence; but at its close, the influx of foreign-born people set in with increased velocity. Mr. Young, in the absence of exact figures, estimates the number coming during the period beginning with 1790 and ending with 1820, at 225,000. A very large majority of these were Irish, as is acknowledged by all. They were driven away principally by the unsuccessful rising of 1798, and many other causes. Hence it is that we find them largely represented on land and sea in the war with Great Britain which began in June, 1812, and ended with the battle of New Orleans in February, 1815. The hero of that war, Andrew Jackson, was said to have been born in Ireland when he became a candidate for President of the United States. However that may be, his parentage and personal predilections were unmistakably Irish-born and racy of the Green Isle.

Between 1820 and 1872, the aggregate number of immigrants into the United States is reported at about 8,000,000. Of these, 3,000,000 are accredited to Ireland. But that this proportion is too small is evident from the fact that, until within a few years past, when the strong current of German immigration began to set in, the great majority of all immigrants were Irish. Of course, there are given to Great Britain, *not specified* (as to nationality), 544,000; and, inasmuch as almost the whole immigration from Great Britain for many years was from Ireland alone, we may set down most of these as natives of that island. The proportionate emigration from Ireland during the last fifty years is marked as follows: from 1820 to 1830, 27,106; 1831 (January

1) to 1840, 29,188; 1841 to 1850, 162,332; 1851 to 1860, 748,740; 1861 to 1870, 650,000.

Referring to the value of immigration to the United States, Mr. Young writes as follows:

"Deducting the women and children, who pursue no occupation, about 46 per cent. of the whole immigration have been trained to various pursuits. Nearly half of these are skilled laborers and workmen who have acquired their trades under the rigorous system which prevails in the Old World, and come here to give us the benefit of their training and skill, without repayment of the cost of such education. Nor are the farm laborers and servants destitute of the necessary training to fit them for their several duties; while those classed as common or unskilled laborers are well qualified to perform the labor required, especially in the construction of works of internal improvement. Nearly 10 per cent. consist of merchants and traders, who, doubtless, bring with them considerable capital as well as mercantile experience; while the smaller number of professional men and artists, embracing architects, engineers, inventors, men of thorough training and high order of talent, contribute to our widely extended community not only material, but artistic, æsthetic, intellectual, and moral wealth.

"With regard to the ages of these immigrants, only 25 per cent. are under fifteen years of age, and less than 15 per cent. over forty, leaving upward of 60 per cent. who are in the prime of life at the time of their arrival, ready to enter at once into their several industrial pursuits.

"As to the proportion which subsists between the two sexes, it appears that, as might have been expected, the number of the males largely preponderates over the females. This proportion varies with the different nationalities, the females constituting, as has been stated, with the Chinese, only 7 per cent., while of the Irish it is over 45 per cent., and of the whole number about 40 per cent."

He then goes into a friendly discussion with other writers on statistics as to what is the value in cash to the country of each immigrant. After very properly stating that it is hardly proper or commendable to estimate a human life on the basis of a *cash* valuation, he resumes by saying that, with all respect to those who claim that one thousand dollars may be taken as the average value to the country of each arriving immigrant, eight hundred dollars would be more correct. Even on this basis, he says that the aggregate addition to the wealth of the nation in the year 1871 alone would be $285,000,000; while during the last half-century, it would be $6,243,000,000.

From this estimate it may easily be judged what has been the value to the United States of the constant stream of Irish emigration during the last one hundred years.

CHAPTER III.

ON THE RESOURCES OF THE UNITED STATES—PRESENT OPPORTUNITIES FOR IMMIGRANTS SUPERIOR TO PAST.

TWENTY years ago, it almost cost even healthy persons their lives to cross the Atlantic. It was the actual death of immense numbers. The poor emigrant was simply an article of trade; and the prince-merchants and ship-owners of those times reaped a rich harvest of gain from the violent disruption of Irish society consequent upon the famine of 1846 and 1847. It was the terrible wrenching of a poor and ill-provided people from their native homes, and casting them upon the world unprovided almost in everything, except in badly managed emigrant-ships, in which cruelty to the *mere Irish* ceased to be a sin. There were many exceptions to this, of course; but, as a rule, the truth of the statement defies contradiction. An English philanthropist, Vere Foster, deserves the universal gratitude of his fellow-men, and of none more than of Irishmen, for his noble efforts in preventing the emigrant-ships of twenty years ago from being mere charnel-houses to those who were necessitated to take passage in them. The more effectually to attain his object, he once took a steerage passage in one of those vessels; and his experience on board, having fully justified his previous views upon the subject, enabled him to inaugurate measures of relief for the poor emigrant, which have been acted upon with the best results.

It is no longer either so dangerous or so toilsome a task to cross the Atlantic as it once was. The legislatures both of England and of America have taken important steps to abolish the most flagrant abuses of the emigration system; and the very competition now existing between rival lines of steamers turns to the advantage of the emigrant.

But it is not merely the facilities of crossing the Atlantic that have increased; but, what is more important still, the facilities of making a home on this side of it. The whole country is now checkered with railroads; and one of them actually spans the continent—making a link of iron between the shores of the Atlantic and those of the Pacific. The advantages thus accruing to the American people in general, and to the immigrant portion of them in particular, are incalculable.* Forty years ago, it was a more sad and dismal fate than we

* Since the year 1848, when there were but about 6,000 miles of completed railroad in the country, the railroad system of the United States had increased, on January 1, 1873, to 71,000 miles in actual operation, with 8,000 more in process of construction. The railroad statistics show that in 1858 there were 27,000 miles of roads built, in 1869, 35 000 miles, and that since the war the half of the whole has been constructed and put in operation. The average railroad growth for the last five years has been nearly 6,000 miles annually. At a rate of $40,000 per mile, the cost of the completed roads would be perhaps $3,000,000,000, while those in progress and not yet completed will reach $320,000,000.

can at present realize for a poor immigrant to transport himself and those depending upon him to the vast and unbroken forests of the West. There was little to cheer him on the way, and scarcely a ground of hope for a return. Besides, the want of such civilizing influences as churches and schools made it difficult to retain for any long time the rudest elements of civilized life. All this is changed in our day; and, not to speak of the older States, it is quite true to say that even the remote Territories are fairly supplied with the essential appliances of civilized life.

The blank and dreary horror of never again returning among the scenes and friends of early youth is also greatly diminished. From Chicago and St. Louis to New York, it now takes less than two days in time and not more than twenty-five dollars in money; and from San Francisco, the trip is made in six or seven days, at a *total* expense of about one hundred and fifty dollars. The inference is plain that the emigrant of to-day has many advantages over his predecessor of some years back.

But the advantages here alluded to are trifling when compared with the increased facilities of obtaining good and cheap land in every State and Territory of the Union. The proper development of this subject is a matter of the utmost importance, not only to those who have not yet come, but also to those who, having come, made the great mistake, owing, doubtless, to causes apparently beyond their control, of remaining in the large cities of the Eastern or Western States. To my mind, the all-important want with these people is the want of correct and reliable information regarding the price of land, its particular products, wages, etc.; and that want should be supplied either by official documents of the different States and Territories, or by those whose residence in a particular place for a number of years, and whose character for intelligence and disinterestedness, entitle them to a hearing. It is probable that there is a sufficient number of foreign-born citizens in every State and Territory to obtain an official statement such as I have suggested; and, in the matter of private information, I suppose the numerous Irish-American and Catholic newspapers will give every encouragement to correspondents such as described, and will make their valuable information accessible to all their readers. It appears plain, at least, that all who are, or who aspire to be, leaders and directors of thought among Irish people ought to make of this subject a specialty.

I know there are many who do not admit present opportunities to be equal to past. But what has been already advanced contains a satisfactory answer. Besides, let us, in a brief way, consider the vast extent of the country. According to the official statistics of 1870, thirty-seven States and twelve organized Territories constitute what is known as the United States. The thirty-seven States have an area of one million nine hundred thousand square miles, or an extent of territory sixteen times as large as that of Great Britain and Ireland, which is one hundred and twenty thousand square miles. The same States contain, by the census of 1870, only thirty-eight millions of souls; whereas, the population of Great

Britain and Ireland amounts to thirty-one and a half millions. Even allowing that the land of the United States is no more than one-fourth as productive as that of Britain, still it would be capable of supporting four times the population of that nation. But in this calculation, nothing has been said about the twelve Territories, which will one day be sovereign States, and which cover an area of one million six hundred thousand square miles, with a population of only six hundred thousand souls.

It is manifest that in every State, even the oldest and most thickly inhabited, there is still much room for agricultural pursuits and a certainty of liberal remuneration. For instance, New York State, containing forty-seven thousand square miles, almost as many as England, has a population of only four million four hundred thousand. We also see that, out of an area of twenty-one millions of acres in New York, seven millions still remain unimproved. But if this be true of New York, it applies with *greater* force to nearly all of the other States, and to all the Territories.

Thus far, nothing has been said in regard to what is known as the "Public lands of the United States." This means such portions of States and Territories as have never yet been "entered" or purchased from the Government. These lands are to be found in almost every State, but more especially in the Western States, and in all the Territories. From the beginning of the country to the present time, public lands have been held at the rate of one dollar and twenty-five cents an acre. This entitles the purchaser to a clear title for all time to the land that he pays for. But, on the 1st of January, 1863, an act was passed in the Congress of the United States, by which any citizen of the country, or any person who had declared his intention to become a citizen, might "enter," at a cost of *ten dollars*, one hundred and sixty acres of public land, and obtain for himself and his heirs for ever a valid title to such land, on the condition of *actually* living upon it for five years after making the entry. This law is called the "Homestead Law," and reflects infinite credit upon the legislators of America. It more than realizes the highest dreams of the most *ultra* communists of this or any other age. But the condition of actual residence on the land saves the law from the imputation of wild theory, because it means that a man must *work* if he wishes to have a home. An important remark is in place here; it is drawn from the perusal of all the pamphlets on immigration written in this country, and from the most experienced observers of immigrant life. It is that, when it is possible, several families, who are acquainted with one another, ought to emigrate together, and settle in the same place. The advantages of even two or three such families or individuals settling together are known to be very great.

CHAPTER IV.

ON THE KIND OF PERSONS WHO OUGHT TO EMIGRATE.

MECHANICS, laborers, farmers, or men of business, who are in a prosperous condition where they are, ought not to think of emigrating. Speaking of the first two classes, I mean, of course, those only who have a prospect of making independent homes; those who cannot acquire *homes of their own* in one part of the United States by honest industry, frugality, and sobriety, ought to go where they can. The difficulty of doing it in all large cities is increased tenfold, when the high rents and high prices of the common necessaries of life are considered. Thus, for instance, in the city of New York, no laborer or mechanic can get a decent room or two in a *tenement-house* under twelve or fifteen dollars a month. Such persons, beginning life without any capital, as we may suppose, in most cases, can hardly be expected ever to rise to independence. It is clear and undeniable that men of the same class have gone either to the smaller towns of the West and South, or to the country parts, and have acquired their own homes in every case in which steadiness in work and sobriety justified the hope of their doing so.

Speaking of emigration from the old countries of

Europe, it is well to remark that young people, from the ages of fifteen to twenty-five, are entirely more calculated to succeed than persons of a more advanced age. The customs and manners of all countries and of every people are different; and old people, or even those of the middle state of life, are seldom so easily brought into the customs of strangers as young people. Besides, it is natural to suppose that the affections of persons somewhat advanced in years for their native place are much stronger than those of young people; and the rupture of the ties which bind them to home is consequently attended with more pain. I have known many an aged father and mother, who, although having the kindest and the best children in the world to greet their landing in America, rarely, if ever, became reconciled to their lot. The familiar scenes and associations of from fifty to seventy years are lost; and no amount of novelty in the change of circumstances can fill up the blank caused thereby in the affections of the heart. If it were not for the deep religious sentiment which seems to be inherent in our race, much more discontent and despondence would prevail among old people who emigrate than we now meet with. It is well to remark, however, that the unfitness for emigration mentioned herein does not generally prevail to any great extent among Americans, or among people who have lived in America for any number of years.

CHAPTER V.

THE VOYAGE AND THE LANDING—CASTLE GARDEN AND WARD'S ISLAND, NEW YORK.

YOUNG persons, then, having made up their minds to emigrate, ought to begin by a religious preparation. If they are Catholics—and to these I principally address myself, because they are entirely the most numerous among English-speaking emigrants—they ought to receive worthily the sacraments of the church before leaving home. All Catholics know that this is a duty incumbent upon them in all undertakings involving danger, and also in entering upon a new condition of life. An unburdened conscience gives a man the freedom of heaven, and establishes him in peace with God and his fellow-men.

In purchasing tickets, care should be taken that the agent applied to is authorized to sell them; and if the ticket is what is called a *through ticket*—that is, one that gives the holder a passage to some city or railway station in the interior of the country—he should make enquiry only of some authorized person as to the best means of reaching his place of destination. If the landing is made at New York, there can be no difficulty in this particular, because the officers of the Board of Emigration at Castle Garden will furnish all such information gratis.

On the voyage, it is very injurious to enter into sharp disputes on subjects relating to religion or politics. Generally, these matters of dispute are solved according to the feelings, prejudices, and education of each individual; and the greatest amount of wrangling cannot change the conviction of any one. Conversation must be had on board, of course, but let it be in a friendly, quiet manner; and if one man can get information from another that will be of use to him in the country to which he is travelling, it matters little what is the religion or political opinion of the friend who imparts it.

No unnecessary delay should be made at the place of landing; it involves a loss of time and of money, and begets disgust and embarrassment. If the emigrant is to go to the West or South, or to the country parts in the neighborhood of New York, the sooner he gets there, the better.

A word respecting Castle Garden and Ward's Island is in place here. They are distinct departments of the same institution, both being controlled by the COMMISSIONERS OF IMMIGRATION OF THE STATE OF NEW YORK. This Commission entered upon its career of usefulness in the year 1848, with Gulian C. Verplanck, a true friend of the immigrant, as its first President. It is not now what it was at first, circumstances and experience requiring or suggesting some new regulation or improvement every year. It is essentially an institution of protection to the immigrant. It is as truly a work of mercy as a hospital or an orphan asylum. Not that the funds for its support come from the State or from private charity; on the contrary, they are contributed by the immigrant himself, by a tax of one dollar and fifty cents on every one that arrives, which is paid out of his passage-money; but the application of this money for the guidance and protection of the immigrant is a real benefit to him and to the country.

All immigrants are obliged to land at Castle Garden, where they are provided with temporary accommodations suitable to their requirements. Those who have tickets for the interior, or money to take them to any point outside of New York, are immediately put upon one or other of the great railroad lines diverging from that city to all parts of the country, without any trouble or risk to the immigrant. The principal railroads have offices in Castle Garden, where the tickets may be procured without the necessity of going to seek them in the city. Any immigrants having gold, silver, or uncurrent money of any kind can have it changed into the current money of the United States, also, at Castle Garden. The rate of exchange is exactly the rate allowed at the best banking-houses.

Ward's Island is the place to which are sent all immigrants who, having neither money nor friends, are sent there until they are provided with suitable employment. All immigrants sick on landing are cared for in the kindest manner at the hospital on Ward's Island; and even such as get sick before they have become citizens of the United States are received on their own or their friends' application.

Most of those brought to Ward's Island leave it in a few days, having been put in communication with their friends or provided with situations. Through the kindness of Mr. Bernard Casserly, the indefatigable Superintendent of Immigration, I have before me the Reports of the Commissioners for the years 1871 and 1872, from which it appears that 31,384 persons were provided with employment during the year 1871, and 32,592 in 1872. Taken all in all, it must be admitted by every unprejudiced mind that the work of the Commission during the quarter of a century of its existence reflects the greatest credit upon the individuals composing it and upon the country, the genius of whose institutions inspired a work of such practical utility.

Lately there are rumors afloat to the effect that the United States Government is making efforts to assume control of this institution. Many, especially those in the shipping interests, seem to advocate the policy. Some even speak disparagingly of the efforts of the Commissioners to secure the protection and comfort of the immigrant. Whilst acknowledging everything human to be susceptible of improvement, it seems clear to any honest mind that the Commission of Immigration of the State of New York is the best institution of the kind in the world, and has adhered as faithfully to its professed purposes as any reasonable man can expect. The threat, therefore, of its abolition forebodes a real calamity. If, for instance, we allow ourselves to imagine that no such institution existed during the last twenty-five years, what untold misery, degradation, and general demoralization, not only of immigrants, but also of those who would have lived by cheating and deceiving them, meet our view! Those who wish to know the cruel treatment of immigrants from the beginning of American colonization to a period reaching back only a few years are referred to *Kapp on Immigration* for facts and statistics startling and shocking in the last degree. I know that the General Government has made many laudable efforts for the benefit and protection of the immigrant, but nothing so practically beneficial has yet appeared as the institution consisting of Castle Garden and Ward's Island, New York.

CHAPTER VI.

ON EMPLOYMENT AND ECONOMY.

THE importance of this chapter to emigrants and their children can not be over-estimated. It contains the secret of success or failure. And *first*, as to employment. Young persons from the ages of 12 to 20 years can select in America almost any trade or profession for which they consider themselves fit. Older people ought to adhere to the trade or occupation to which they have been accustomed from early life. Thus, for instance, the majority of Irish people have been accustomed to agricultural labor; and to abandon it in America is, in most cases, the certain road to poverty and dependence. It is quite true to say that farming is not carried on in the same manner in America as it is in Ireland; but an Irish or English farmer or farm-laborer is sure to learn the American system of farming much sooner than he can anything else; and the system is so simple withal that diligence in it is the certain road to success. Small capitalists from Europe or the Eastern cities would do well, before investing their money in farms in the West or South, to hire for a year with persons already settled in those parts, and thus practically acquire the peculiar knowledge requisite in this pursuit. A thorough knowledge of farming in the Northern States may be acquired in this time easily. And I have known persons in the Southern States, who had lived in cities before the late Civil War, as grocers or men of business, to go out into the country, take up land, and successfully raise cotton and all other products congenial to that part of the country. I well remember the profound and practical truths uttered by these men when they said: "What are our people doing with themselves; when instead of coming here and taking up this land, where it is so cheap (from $5 to $20 an acre *for ever*), they rather cling to the great cities, and there expose their children to every species of immorality; and where they live from hand to mouth, without the least hope of rising to independence?" This particular point of men following the occupation to which they are most adapted cannot be dwelt upon too much. And hence, for the same reason that I would advise a man brought up to agriculture in Ireland to stick to it in America, I would also advise the mechanic to follow *his* trade; and although the carpenter, mason, or blacksmith may find his business carried on a little differently in America from the manner of old countries, still, as a man of sense, he will conform his method to what he finds going on around him, and be successful in the end. The reason that so much stress is laid upon the subject of procuring land is very plainly laid down in the first and second chapters, where the advantages of the present time in this particular are so clearly pointed out.

Whether persons have been brought up to cultivate the land or not, it will do them no harm to get land, now that it is so cheap in most places outside the large cities.

There is in it the foundation of independence. Of course, land, like all things else, should be purchased with judgment and common sense; and no steps should be taken recklessly or without counsel.

The subject of economy or saving is so near akin to that of employment or earning that both should come under the same heading. In fact, it is not much use to speak of producing, if the genius of destroying or wasting be not excluded; and it may truly be said that one of the saddest chapters in the history of Irish life in America is the chapter of reckless squandering. Every one that thinks of it must remember in his lifetime numbers, even of laborers, who, if they had been *moderately* saving, might have been independent. Many a mechanic, to my knowledge, has been able to earn from three to six dollars a day, and at the end of the year had saved nothing. Reckless waste is the bane of the working-classes in America. Its correction, in one form or another, is the greatest benefit that can be conferred upon American society. Courageous and manly self-denial, which is one of the greatest of the Christian virtues, is the only remedy for this evil. This self-denial should begin with the head of the family; his example to his wife and children is all-powerful. Let us suppose, for instance, that a mechanic in one of the cities or towns of America finds, on examining the subject, that he has unnecessarily spent, on an average, 50 cents every day in tobacco or drink. Fifty cents a day makes, in the year, one hundred and eighty-two dollars and fifty cents. Let us call it, for convenience, two hundred dollars.

Now, by actual calculation, this sum, put at interest at 6 per cent. per annum, which is a low rate of interest in the United States, doubles itself, if the interest is not drawn, in twelve years. In twenty-five years, it becomes the important sum of eight hundred and fifty-eight dollars. Let us again suppose a laboring man on the railroads or elsewhere, getting one dollar and a half or two dollars a day; he can easily save of this amount twenty-seven and a half cents. This amounts to one hundred dollars in three hundred and sixty-five days; and if placed at interest, as before stated, will amount in twelve years to two hundred dollars, and in twenty-five years to four hundred and twenty-nine dollars.* It has been accurately ascertained that a boy or girl, who at the age of fourteen, saves two and three-fourth cents every day, placing it at interest in the manner stated, will be worth two thousand nine hundred dollars at the age of sixty-four years. A saving of twenty-seven and a half cents a day amounts, in the same period of fifty years, to the sum of twenty-nine thousand dollars. One of the worst signs of the times in America in our days is a restless and insatiable desire to become rich in a short while. To this desire is sacrificed peace of mind, health of body, and even honor and honesty itself. And it often happens that riches suddenly acquired are as quickly lavished, either in gambling, drinking, or foolish speculation. According to the suggestions laid down in this chapter, it is evident that even a labor-

* But if this is the result of one year's saving, what will it be in ten or twenty years?

er, or a poor working-boy or girl in the factories, can save enough to keep them decently in old age, if they have a mind to do it. Eagerness to become suddenly rich is a sin; and, generally, it cannot be done except at the expense of our own honesty and our neighbors' property.* Servant-girls in America get from eight to sixteen dollars a month—sometimes they get as high as twenty. Now, if they save half of that amount every year, and place it at interest, they will have acquired a considerable sum at the end of ten years. Many of them, to my certain knowledge, have, in the course of twenty or thirty years, by faithful industry and moderate economy, become owners of from three to five thousand dollars. Be it understood that the object of the writer is not to destroy or warp any of the grand and beautiful traits of character in our race for which they are distinguished all over the world. Filial devotion, love of friends, and readiness to relieve their wants, are characteristics of our race that deserve all honor. I do not think, however, that what is contained herein will interfere with, but rather foster, those noble virtues. Anyhow, the fact is undeniable that the want of a moderate economy in our people has caused much suffering among them, and has often resulted in the ruin of body and soul.

In regard to placing money in savings-banks, it is well to remark that inexperienced persons ought to con-

* There are many cases, owing to the great progress of the country, in which men become wealthy in a short time without sacrificing principle. This is accidental, however.

sult a clergyman or some well-informed friend before depositing their money; because it is unhappily but too well known that many such banks have failed in various places, leaving those who trusted in their solvency penniless. It may be well to state, moreover, that, in regard to saving, the most effectual and profitable way is to invest in a farm or in town lots. In America, there is always time given in which to pay for these; and the necessity of meeting the deferred payments stimulates industry and produces economy.

I cannot close this chapter without saying a word on the subject of what are called "strikes." It means a combination of mechanics or laborers, in which they refuse to work, except the wages are increased or the hours of labor are reduced. In some cases it involves both, in others only one or another, of these conditions. It is the old contest between labor on the one side and capital on the other. The best-informed and most experienced mechanics and laborers that I have met have been unanimous in saying that, although societies having for their object the mutual protection of the members are good, and are a salutary stay upon the tyranny of capital, still, as a general thing, "strikes" are injurious to the working-man. Thus, in a "strike," a man may be kept idle for a month or two by the rules of the society, and the increased wages that is looked for may not be sufficient to make up for the loss of that month's wages in a year. Besides, in many instances, "strikes" have paralyzed and broken up prosperous business enterprises.

I do not wish to say more upon this subject; but I know for certain that, outside of large cities, "strikes" cannot take place with much effect; and that, when we consider this as a free country, labor of all kinds will, in the long run, be free.

CHAPTER VII.

ON THE SUBJECT OF EDUCATION—GOOD AND BAD READING.

IT is cheering to know that most of the emigrants from Ireland of the present time are educated, at least in the elementary branches. Many are thoroughly educated, and expect, not unreasonably of course, to get what are called " situations " in which their knowledge can be turned to account. As a general thing, these situations can rarely be obtained, except by the influence of some opulent friend, and especially if that friend is in business himself. It is a very false policy for a young man, therefore, to count much upon the accidental turning up of "situations," when, if he has ordinary health, he can get good wages at almost any kind of manual labor. In many places, clerkships, etc., are filled by the relatives or special acquaintances of the men in business. Of course, it is also true that many of the most eminent lawyers, physicians, literary and business men, in the United States are of our race; each individual of these has a peculiar history of his own; and that history will be repeated by many another man or boy now in obscurity. I am, therefore, only speaking for the larger number, even of scholars, who, if they cannot turn their scholarship to account, ought to take up some other honest way of living.

But the primary object of this chapter is to awaken thought in regard to the absolute necessity of at least a primary education among our people. By this I mean reading, writing, spelling, arithmetic, and, if possible, English grammar. Every one emigrating to America, and every child born in America, ought to be supplied with this amount of knowledge at the very least. In regard to grown persons, or young people who are obliged to work, if they are deficient in this knowledge, they ought to supply the defect by going to night-school, or in some other way.

Again, the condition of the Irish race in this century is most singular and exceptional. Probably one-half of all the people born on Irish soil during the last fifty years have left their native homes, and are now either dead or scattered over the nations of the earth. Ignorance, therefore, of the elementary sciences would deprive one-half of the race of all proper and natural means of communication with the other. I say *proper* and *natural,* because members of the same family, or even near relatives or warm friends, cannot, without great inconvenience, employ strangers to write their letters. Oftentimes something has to be written that should not be known outside the family circle; and, in such cases, it becomes very irksome and disagreeable to be obliged to let outsiders know it. If the simplest rudiments of learning were useful only in this respect, it would amply repay all the pains and expense required in mastering them. But at present there is ample opportunity of attaining this knowledge; and parents are most inexcusable if they neglect their children in this particular. Eighty years ago, it was a penal offence, according to English law, for Catholics to teach or be taught the rudest elements of literature; this system of law has happily broken down of its own weight, and we are now on equal footing with all other English-speaking people in our right to obtain a thorough education. Our fathers deserve all praise in this particular, because, in order to obtain the education forbidden to them at home, they either transported themselves beyond the seas, or betook themselves to the "hedge-schools" of Ireland. Our chances, therefore, being so much superior to theirs, we are inexcusable if we do not turn them to account.

In regard to reading, it is a fact well proved that nothing advances so much the morality of families and individuals as a supply of good books. Over sermons they have the advantage that the sermon, once heard, may be forgotten and never heard again; but the ideas contained in the book may be recurred to again and again. Therefore, all heads of families ought to impose it upon themselves, as a matter of serious obligation, to supply their children according to their means with good books. Young men and women ought to provide themselves, also, with good Catholic works. The amount of drunkenness, debauchery, evil language, and detraction prevented by good reading is incalculable. Many a time I have met men of the highest respectability in their respective localities, men of wealth and standing, kind to the poor and generous to the church, who frankly acknowledged to me that all they were worth in the world was owing to the practice adopted in early youth of reading good books.

While on this subject, it may be well to call attention to the great progress of our English Catholic literature in the present century. Towards the close of the last century, it was forbidden by the laws, already alluded to, to print, publish, or read Catholic books. To-day (1873) there are in the British Empire at least ten large Catholic publishing houses, and in the United States about fifteen. The number and excellence of the works published by these twenty-five houses mark a new era in the history of English literature. A literature which, for three centuries, was so hostile to our race and creed—a literature, withal, that we were forbidden to take part in—now begins to acknowledge, slowly indeed, but surely, the injustice donetous, and the reasonableness of our claims to public consideration. This result is mainly due to the unflinching courage and to the eminent ability of our writers and lecturers during the last seventy years. The conclusion from these remarks is that every man, and woman, and child of our race and creed ought to purchase and read, according to their means and time, some of the admirable works that are being published every day. Every parish ought to have a circulating library; because, inasmuch as it is an age of reading and enquiry, and as bad books will be read by the young if good ones are not accessible, it follows that every person alive to Catholic interests should take some part in the good work.

This is the proper place to mention a few, at least, of the works most likely to be useful to those I am addressing. But inasmuch as most of the works published are excellent, each in its own way, it seems difficult to call attention to any without speaking of all. Works, however, that are stamped with the favorable verdict of time and universal acceptance may be noticed. *The Following* (*or Imitation*) *of Christ*, *The Memorial of a Christian Life*, *The Commandments and Sacraments*, *The Devout Life*, *The Catholic Christian Instructed*, *The Way of Salvation*, *Familiar Discourses to the Young*, *The Guide to Catholic Young Women*, may be set down as among the best. These works are generally published in a convenient size, and are very cheap.

CHAPTER VIII.

ON THE CHURCH AND THE DUTIES OF RELIGION.

ALTHOUGH the present work does not profess to be one of a peculiarly religious character, yet the eminently religious feeling of those to whom it is addressed—a feeling, indeed, which seems to be a part of their nature—justifies a few words on the subject of religion.

In the outset, one feels inclined to give at least a short history of the wonderful progress of the Catholic religion in the United States, commencing at the Revolution. But it is impossible in a work like this, and there are many publications easily obtained in which the want is supplied. Suffice it here to say that on the 15th of August, 1790, eighty-three years ago, the first bishop of the United States was consecrated in Lulworth Castle, England, the residence of one of the old Catholic families of that country. This bishop was JOHN CARROLL, of Maryland—a name distinguished by all who bore it in the American Revolution for patriotism, honor, and devotion to the cause of liberty. When he returned in the December following to his see of Baltimore, he found himself the only bishop of the whole United States of that day, having under his jurisdiction twenty-five priests and from twenty-five to forty thousand people. The residence of these was principally confined to Maryland and Pennsylvania. In 1808, eighteen years later, bishops were appointed to New York, Philadelphia, Boston, and Bardstown, Kentucky. The Catholic population then amounted to about one hundred and fifty thousand souls.

In 1850, we find twenty-seven bishops, with a population of about one and a half million. At the present time (1873), the Catholic population cannot fall short of six millions, or about one-sixth of the entire population of the country. Allowing their number to have been forty thousand in 1790, it would have been only one-seventieth part of the population of that time. This wonderful increase is owing in some degree to the acquisition of the vast territory west of the Alleghany Mountains, where there were a few French settlements, and to the cession of New Mexico and California after the Mexican War of 1847; but it is mainly due to the constant stream of Irish emigration during the last seventy years. Of course, there has been a large emigration of Germans during the same period, and especially during the last fifteen years; but this will not change the truth of what has been stated, inasmuch as many of the German immigrants are either of no religious profession, or else do not belong to the Catholic Church.

Differences of religion do not count for much, in a temporal point of view, among Americans of the genuine type. An honest man who firmly adheres to his religious principles, and is sober and industrious withal, is certain to obtain the respect of all his neighbors in

America, no matter how much they may differ with him in his religious belief. Since the time of the Revolution, there has no been *ascendency* party here either in church or in state; but a perfect equality prevails, and even a possibility, where there is a fitness, to enjoy any office of honor or trust. Foreign-born citizens are eligible to any office in the land, excepting only the office of President of the United States.

The wonderful progress of the Catholic Church, therefore, and the spirit of generous devotedness displayed by Catholics in raising magnificent churches all over the land, is a matter of admiration among Americans of every religious opinion. Often non-Catholics show the greatest liberality in helping to build and decorate our churches.

I wish to call special attention here to a remarkable fact. Wherever, among the Catholics of America, you find good churches, beautifully or decently fitted up for divine worship, there you invariably find a thrifty and prosperous Catholic people. Wherever, on the contrary, you find a poor and wretched church structure, due regard being paid to the number of the congregation, you almost as certainly find a people given up to drunkenness and other degrading vices. God blesses generosity directed to himself an hundredfold. In some places, and under certain circumstances, it often seems a gigantic project to build a good church; but if we analyze the subject, the difficulty vanishes. Let us take, for instance, a Catholic population, either in the towns or country parts, of two hundred families; this number of families is supposed to consist of ten or twelve hundred persons. Supposing they want to build a church costing twenty-five thousand dollars; if each family contribute, on an average, one hundred and twenty-five dollars, the work is accomplished. Supposing, moreover, that this sum is contributed in five equal annual instalments of twenty-five dollars each, or even in work upon the building, the burden is lightened, and the result is the same. So, also, a population of one hundred families, wishing to build a church costing ten thousand dollars, can do it by each family contributing one hundred dollars. In all contributions of this nature, the principal point is that the burden be borne by all according to their means. It is generally the case in these matters that while some are more liberal than can reasonably be expected, others keep aloof from the performance of their duty, and claim it as a right, nevertheless, to grumble and complain respecting the work that is done, and the way in which it is done.

A word of recognition is here due to the bishops and priests of the United States; for, in the whole history of Christianity, I hardly think we can find a priesthood so devoted to duty, and so laborious in the work of building churches, schools, orphan asylums, academies, and hospitals, as in this country. So great has been the energy displayed, and the indomitable perseverance under all kinds of difficulties, that our clergy have attracted the attention and won the admiration of all who have formed their acquaintance, irrespective of race or creed.

A few words, also, may be in place respecting the

duties of religion. One of the most powerful means of preserving the faith, and of leading a virtuous life, is the frequent and worthily receiving the sacraments of the church. The writer is acquainted with many cases in which non-Catholic employers—masters and mistresses—will have no servants excepting *Catholics* who comply with the duties of their religion. It is probably needless to say that every Catholic is obliged to receive the sacraments at least once a year, and this at the time of Easter. In the present condition of things in this country, hardly any one can be excused from complying with this duty. Churches and priests are now sufficiently numerous to give to all the opportunity of receiving the sacraments. Even if it should cost a journey of twenty-five or fifty miles once or twice a year, it is worth all the trouble. There are also among us several organized bands of missionary priests; and the amount of good effected by their labors is incalculable. Any one living within the reach of a *mission* ought to avail himself of the benefits thereby held out to him. Fathers and mothers of families should see to it in time that their children are thoroughly instructed in the principles of their faith, and prepared for first communion at a proper age. Children allowed to grow up without religion are a curse to society, and to no members of society so much as to their own parents. Parents of the wealthier classes are greatly mistaken if, in sending their children to school, they do not provide for their religious instruction. It is the basis of all moral, social, and domestic excellence; and if made light of in youth, parents will live long enough to repent of their folly when it is too late.

There have been many converts to the Catholic faith in the United States from the beginning of the present century. A fair proportion of these have been persons of eminent ability, and have filled the highest offices in church and state. It is a fact, nevertheless, altogether undeniable, that great numbers of emigrants and their children have been lost to the faith, all over the land, on account of the absence of clergymen, the fewness of churches, and the social or family alliances frequently entered into. The Catholic population is now probably six or seven millions; but, if all the Catholic emigrants of the last two hundred years had had even moderate opportunities of exercising their religious belief, it would, doubtless, be three times that number.

CHAPTER IX.

ON TEMPERANCE.

MUCH, of late years, has been spoken and written upon the subject of drunkenness in its evil effects upon the family and upon society; and, in truth, too much can not be said against this most degrading vice. To me it has always appeared that Father Mathew, whose name is a synonym for temperance, was the greatest benefactor of his race and of mankind in modern times. Millions now living, if not in opulence, at least in independent circumstances and enjoying the comfort of peaceful homes, are indebted to him for all they possess. Among a people to whom a wicked system of government, and false ideas regarding the requirements of social life, made it *honorable* to be a drunkard, Father Mathew raised his voice against the prevailing sin. He labored for years in the good work; and although that work may be criticised, and has been without justice or discrimination, still we must conclude that the blessed voice of the Apostle of Temperance was not stilled in death until he had convinced his countrymen that drunkenness was a *dishonor* and a *disgrace* to all Christian men. Like all true reformers, he undertook to reform ideas first, knowing that the reformation of society would follow.

But to our subject: It is well to remark that no one can justly lay to the charge of our race a greater propensity to strong drink than is manifested by people of other nationalities. This would be foolish and absurd. But there is among us a social and convivial spirit which, if not kept within due bounds, is apt to result in excesses of which no one ever dreamed. Hence the necessity of a word of warning. A young man beginning life, and finding himself thrown in the society of persons habituated to excessive drinking, must cut loose from that society, no matter what it may cost him; because, if he does not drink too much himself, he will be annoyed by those who do; and if he does drink too much, he will contract a habit in a short time that will lead to certain ruin. The graphic pictures drawn by the ablest men of our race regarding this sin and its evil effects I will not attempt to condense or quote; all that need be said upon it here is that the *society* of the intemperate must be avoided by all who wish to keep temperate.

In regard to the unfortunate class who have contracted the evil habit, it is necessary to say that all the power of reason and religion must be brought to bear upon them to effect a reformation. It is necessary to reflect that, even as men possessed of freedom, we cannot be forced against our will to do what is wrong in regard to ourselves or others; to say so would be to impute to the Almighty himself the greatest tyranny, inasmuch as he gave us laws that we cannot observe. Again, as Christians, we ought to place before our minds our

Lord and Saviour hanging on the cross; that, in his burning thirst, he refused the poor comfort offered to him when they asked him to drink vinegar mixed with gall.

CHAPTER X.

WHERE CAN EMIGRANTS BEST SUCCEED IN OBTAINING HOMES?

THIS is the proper place to point out, in a special manner, those parts of the country in which the poor man is most likely to succeed in procuring a home. Inasmuch as the whole second part of this work is devoted to that subject, I will only make a few brief remarks here.

In the first place, industry, economy, and *health* will secure the poor man a home almost anywhere in the United States outside of the large cities. It has often been accomplished, even within the cities, by steady attention to work. And in the suburbs of all the large cities poor men may generally obtain a home by purchasing ground on a long credit, and putting up a cheap house. The street-cars and other conveyances are generally accessible from every place in cities, and enable persons, for a small sum, to get to their work.

But if we consider the subject of procuring farms of eighty acres and upwards, or of getting property on a large scale in cities or towns, it may be said, without hesitation or fear of contradiction, that the country lying between the Mississippi River on the east and the

Pacific Ocean on the west, and that lying between the Ohio River on the north and the Gulf of Mexico on the south, is the best of all. Let us take, for instance, the PACIFIC COAST—the States of California and Oregon, and the Territory of Washington. Together they cover an area of three hundred and fourteen thousand square miles, or an area five times as large as that of the six New England States, the population of which is three and a half millions, whereas the population of the two Pacific States and one Territory is only six hundred and eighty thousand. Special attention is called to the letters and statistics regarding the Pacific States.

Again, it is certain that large tracts of *Government land* may still be obtained in Minnesota, Nebraska, Kansas, and in all the Territories west and south of them. Railroad lands, as they are called, on account of being owned by railroad companies, may be bought at a cost of from three to twelve dollars an acre, and on *a long credit*, in Iowa, Missouri, Kansas, Nebraska, and generally in all the country west of the Mississippi. Lands lying near railroads have many advantages over those more remote, in the way of markets, churches, schools, etc.

In the SOUTHERN STATES since the late Civil War, owing to the absence or derangement of labor and the pressure of taxation, lands partially or entirely cleared and lying near railroads may be purchased for sums ranging from two to twenty dollars an acre. No lands in the South, excepting those in the near neighborhood of cities, are higher. When large tracts are purchased

in the South for the purpose of colonization, the terms are still more favorable.

I cannot close this chapter without proposing to wealthy Catholics an idea that may be carried out with great benefit to many—injuriously to no one. Effectual action in regard to this idea would more than realize the whole purpose of this work.

Let us suppose one thousand Catholics in the whole United States, owning money or real estate to the amount of from two hundred thousand to one million of dollars; it is certain that at least five hundred of these may be found in the city of New York alone. Let us further suppose that each one of these invests twenty-five thousand dollars in the lands of the West or South at the rate of two dollars and a half per acre. The investment so made would include ten thousand acres of land. This tract, divided by eighty, makes one hundred and twenty-five—the number of farms of that size contained in the tract. This would make a respectable colony, and would put one hundred and twenty-five families on the road to independence. Multiply this number by one thousand, and we have the important figure of one hundred and twenty-five thousand families, or about one million of persons, so settled on land.

Be it distinctly understood that the supposition here is not that these capitalists give away their land for nothing. It is merely that, having possession of a large tract, they may enable poor people to settle upon it, and give them time—say ten or fifteen years—to pay the principal, receiving in the meantime the interest usually given. One great drawback with poor people in settling on land is the danger of a defective title; it often keeps them back when there is no such danger. Now, the very names of honest Catholic capitalists who would make of this enterprise a special object of their lives would furnish a sufficient guarantee against swindling. It is, therefore, clear that a combination, such as suggested, would go far towards settling a large number upon farms of their own who in cities never can rise to even a moderate independence.

Again, in saying that land may be had as low as two dollars and a half per acre, the supposition is that the payment is in *cash*, and with the express object of establishing *colonies*. These two conditions invariably command good terms in the purchase of lands either from the Government or from railroad companies; because cash payments are always desirable, and an increase of population increases taxes for the Government and business for the railroads.

The proposition is distinctly made; who will take it up? There is in it neither danger nor risk; because, even if the land were not sold, it is certain not to depreciate in value, and cannot be anything else than a safe investment. Here is a chance for the exercise of patriotism and love of our fellow-man in the most practical and tangible form; let us hope that some one may lead the way, and that many will follow.

Part Second.

CONTAINING SPECIAL STATISTICS OF THE VARIOUS STATES AND TERRITORIES COMPRISING THE UNITED STATES, GENERAL RESOURCES OF THE SAME, AND CONDITION OF THE CATHOLIC CHURCH IN EACH.

PRELIMINARY REMARKS.

1. The extent, population, and resources of each State and Territory, also the number of foreign-born people of the Irish and German nationalities in each, and the condition of the Catholic Church, will form the subject-matter of this second part.

It will be noticed that the population of 1860, as well as that of 1870, is given; the object being to show, by the increase of population, the States and Territories in which the greatest progress is being made. The increase of population may not, in every particular instance, be an exact test of the advancing prosperity of a country or city; but in this country, where the facilities of travel have made it so easy to move from a less to a more prosperous locality, it is a good test in the great majority of cases.

2. By the census report of 1870, it will be seen that, of the total population of the United States of that date (38,558,371), 5,557,229 were born outside of the United States. Of this number, 1,855,827, or nearly two millions, were born in Ireland, and 1,679,025 in Germany. Of the Irish-born people in the United States, about one-half are in the *three States* of New York, Pennsylvania, and Massachusetts; and 1,217,496 of them are to be found in the six New England States, New York, Pennsylvania, and New Jersey.

Of the 1,690,533 Germans in the United States in

1870, more than one-half are to be found in the four States of New York, Ohio, Illinois, and Wisconsin; or, in exact numbers, 865,871. The greatest number of Germans, besides those mentioned, are still in the Western States.

3. The object of giving the numbers of Germans and Irish in each State and Territory is to show the locality of these two races, which, for years past, have furnished the most considerable part of the emigration to the United States. It will be seen that, while the Irish people seem to cling to the cities and manufacturing States, the Germans proceed in larger numbers to the great States of the West, and apply themselves to the cultivation of the soil. In fact, it seems that many colonies of Germans have come directly from their homes in the Fatherland to Wisconsin and other States of the West, and have settled down at once upon land, without any delay at all at the port of landing. Thus may we account for the great prosperity of the Germans in America. They follow, as nearly as possible, the occupations to which they were accustomed in their own country; and hence the cause of their success.

4. Of the other nationalities in the United States, the English (many of whom are of Irish parentage) form the largest part. The number given is 550,688; of whom the largest numbers are found in the following States: New York (110,000), Pennsylvania (70,000), Illinois (54,000), Ohio (36,000), Michigan (35,000), California (17,000), and the Territory of Utah (16,000). The Scotch in the United States in 1870 number 140,809,

the largest part of whom are found in New York, Pennsylvania, and Illinois. The Welsh are set down as 74,530; and they are principally to be found in Pennsylvania, Ohio, Wisconsin, and New York.

The French in the United States are set down as 116,240, and are found in largest numbers in New York, Ohio, Louisiana, and Illinois. The British American Provinces of Canada, etc., have furnished 490,000 to the population of the United States. Most of these are of Irish, English, or French parentage, and are principally found in Michigan, New York, Massachusetts, Illinois, and Vermont.

5. The statistics thus given are founded upon the *Report of the Ninth Census of the United States*, taken in 1870. The price of land, of labor, etc., as noticed in the following pages, has been found in special reports from the Governors of States and Territories, or from a work entitled *Special Report on Immigration*, prepared by the Hon. Edward Young, Chief of the Bureau of Statistics, Washington, D. C., U. S. To immigrants, or persons intending to emigrate, this is a work of great value. When *Government land* is mentioned, it means such land as may be acquired by the Homestead or Pre-emption titles directly from the Government, in quantities of one hundred and sixty, eighty, or forty acres, according to its nearness to railroads or other public improvements. Generally, I have not made mention of the particular wages given in each State to persons of different avocations; but this defect is supplied by Table No. 1, taken from the United States report, and is entirely reliable.

6. The controversy so frequently raised as to the relative numbers of the Celtic and Anglo-Saxon races in the United States, although of little practical importance, has, for a great number, both of Americans and foreigners, a special interest. In considering the question, it is necesssary to keep in mind the fact that, from the beginning of what is now called the United States, there has been a large intermixture of Celts, both French and Irish, among the English population. The Scotch element, also, is not to be disregarded in this connection, for we find them respectably represented in all the original States. When we reflect that the total population of the country in the year 1800 was only 5,500,000, and that the principal emigration since that date has been Irish—amounting to fully four millions—we may very justly conclude that the Irish and their descendants in the United States number, at the very least, fourteen millions. Adding the French, especially the Canadian French, and Scotch elements of our population to this, the sum total of the Celtic population is not probably short of eighteen millions.

If any calculation of the numbers of the purely Germanic population has been made, I am not aware of it; but, even supposing that the great German emigration dates back only about twenty-five years, it must amount now to seven or eight millions at least.

Then we have about five millions of Africans in all the States, which leaves only ten millions of the Anglo-Saxon race in the United States.

7. It will be noticed that foreigners are very few in the

Southern States, although most of these have a remarkably healthy climate and fertile soil. One reason of this is that in those States slave labor prevailed before the late Civil War. Since the war the principal men of the South have made the greatest efforts to secure a large influx of European immigration. To me it seems that if the large land-holders of that section continue to sell to actual settlers farms of eighty or one hundred and sixty acres, on long time and good terms, a large immigration will soon turn in that direction. Some land-owners in the South have even gone so far as to offer *for nothing* alternate plots of their farms to actual settlers. Although this example may not be extensively followed, it is worthy of consideration.

CHAPTER I.

THE SIX NEW ENGLAND STATES.

MAINE.

THIS State occupies the northeastern part of the United States, and has an area of thirty thousand square miles. Population in 1870, 626,915; in 1860, 578,034. Natives of Ireland in 1870, 15,745; of Germany, 508.

Maine was formerly a part of Massachusetts, but became a separate, sovereign State in March, 1820. It is not generally selected by foreigners as a home, especially on account of the rigor of the climate. Honest industry, however, and perseverance are sure to be crowned with success in this as in other States.

The exports of Maine are principally lumber, lime, and granite. One-third of all the ship-building of the United States is done in this State. The manufacture of woollen and cotton fabrics, also of castings and paper, is extensive. Fisheries flourish in this State.

The Catholic statistics will be given under the heading of New Hampshire.

NEW HAMPSHIRE

lies west of Maine and north of Massachusetts; it has an area of nine thousand two hundred and eighty square miles. Population in 1870, 318,370; in 1860, 326,073. Natives of Ireland in 1870, 12,190; of Germany, 436.

New Hampshire is one of the oldest States of the Union, having been one of the original thirteen States that fought for and won American independence. She ratified the United States Constitution on the 26th of June, 1788.

In regard to the prospects for emigrants in this State, the brief remarks already made in regard to Maine will apply equally well here.

Catholic Statistics of Maine and New Hampshire.

These two States form but one diocese, under the jurisdiction of the Bishop of Portland, Maine.

The statistics, as given in the *Catholic Almanac* of 1873, are as follows: One bishop, residing at Portland; fifty-two priests in both States; fifty-eight churches built, and nine building; nine religious institutions, under the direction of Sisters; twenty Catholic free schools. Catholic population, 80,000.

The labors of the reverend Jesuit fathers among the Indians who formerly inhabited this part of the country are given in a work entitled *Catholic Missious in the United States*, by J. G. Shea—a work full of interesting details.

VERMONT

lies west of New Hampshire, from which it is separated by the Connecticut River. Area, nine thousand and fifty-six square miles. Population in 1870, 330,000; in 1860, 315,000. Natives of Ireland in 1870, 14,080; of Germany, 370. Vermont, formed out of the territory of New York, became a State in 1791.

The climate is very healthy, and is not so cold as that of Maine or New Hampshire. The soil on both sides of the Green Mountains, which traverse the State from north to south, is very fertile and well adapted for grazing. Wool is the chief article of export. Quarrying is carried on extensively.

The following is a letter from the Right Rev. Bishop De Goesbriand, regarding the prospects for emigrants in this State:

BURLINGTON, Jan. 23, 1873.

REV. AND DEAR SIR:

In answer to your letter of enquiry, I am told that improved lands in Vermont sell at an average of $50 per acre, and that laborers get on an average one dollar and a half a day. Emigrants do not seem to direct their course in large numbers this way.

Respectfully and truly yours,

L. DE GOESBRIAND, D.D.,
Bishop of Burlington.

The Catholic statistics are as follows: The diocese of Burlington was established in 1853. It has one bishop, at Burlington, whose jurisdiction extends over the whole State; twenty-six priests and thirteen clerical students in 1873; fifty-two churches built, and four building; three religious institutions. Catholic population, about 34,000.

MASSACHUSETTS,

which is one of the old thirteen States, lies south of New Hampshire and Vermont. Area, 7,800 square miles. The Constitution of the United States was accepted here in 1788. Population, 1870, 1,457,351; in 1860, 1,231,066. Natives of Ireland in 1870, 216,120; of Germany, 13,072.

Massachusetts is the most densely populated State in the Union, having one hundred and eighty-seven persons to the square mile. The river valleys are well adapted to agriculture; but the great wealth of the State consists in her manufactures. Cotton and woolen fabrics, carpets, flax, machinery of all kinds, paper, and shoes are among the principal. In regard to the prospects for immigrants in this State, special attention is called to the letter of the Right Rev. Bishop of Hartford, Connecticut, at the end of this chapter; because what applies to his State applies generally to this. In all departments of business, as well as in the various professions, we find the Irish race fairly represented in Massachusetts.

Catholic Statistics.

There are two dioceses in Massachusetts. One is the Diocese of Boston, founded in 1808; and the other, the Diocese of Springfield, founded in June, 1870.

The DIOCESE OF BOSTON, comprising the eastern part of the State, is in a flourishing condition. The following are the principal statistics: one bishop, residing in Boston; one hundred and fifty priests, and seventy-five clerical students; eighty-seven churches built, and six in course of erection; twenty-six chapels; one college, three female academies; thirteen parochial free schools; three hospitals; six orphan asylums; number of orphans, 600. Catholic population, about 275,000.

The statistics of the DIOCESE OF SPRINGFIELD, which comprises the western counties of the State, are as follows: one bishop, residing at Springfield; sixty-eight priests, and about forty clerical students; sixty-three churches; one college; four convents. Catholic population, about 100,000; making nearly 400,000 Catholics for the State of Massachusetts alone.

RHODE ISLAND

lies south of Massachusetts, and east of Connecticut. It is the smallest State in the Union. It is one of the original thirteen States that struggled for American independence, and ratified the Constitution of the United States in May, 1790.

Its area is only 1,306 square miles. Population in 1870, 217,000; in 1860, 174,620; natives of Ireland in 1870, 31,324; of Germany, 1,201.

Rhode Island is principally a manufacturing State; and the same remarks regarding the prospects of emigrants in Massachusetts apply to this State. A great number of wealthy Irish people, who have carved out large fortunes by honest industry, may be found in this State.

Catholic Statistics.

Providence, although long the residence of the Bishop of Hartford, was not erected into an episcopal see until 1872, when the Right Rev. Bishop McFarland removed to Hartford, Connecticut, and Bishop Hendricken was duly installed as Bishop of Providence.

The new diocese comprises the whole State of Rhode Island and two or three of the counties of Massachusetts bordering upon it. It has one bishop, living in Providence; fifty-three priests, and forty clerical students; forty-three churches built, and five building; six academies—five female and one male. Catholic population, 125,000.

CONNECTICUT

lies south of Massachusetts, and west of Rhode Island. Area, 4,674 square miles. Population in 1870, 537,454; in 1860, 460,147. Natives of Ireland in 1870, 70,630; of Germany, 12,443.

Connecticut is also one of the original thirteen States, and gave her adhesion to the Constitution of the United States in February, 1788.

The river valleys of Connecticut are admirably adapted for agriculture; but manufactures and commerce constitute the principal wealth of the State. The prospects for emigrants are pointed out in the letter of the Right Rev. Bishop McFarland, already referred to.

Catholic Statistics,

The Diocese of Hartford comprises the whole State of Connecticut, and was established in March, 1844. The diocese has one bishop, residing in Hartford; seventy-seven priests, and forty-five clerical students; seventy-six churches built, and nine building; sixty chapels and stations; ten academies—one male and nine female; eighteen Catholic free schools for boys, and nineteen for girls. Catholic population, 140,000.

This makes the whole Catholic population of the six New England States 754,000.

Twenty-five years ago, according to the *Catholic Almanac* of that date (1848), it amounted to only about 80,000 in the diocese of Boston, which comprised the four States of Massachusetts, New Hampshire, Maine, and Vermont; and about 20,000 in the diocese of Hartford, which comprised the States of Rhode Island and Connecticut.

A work of great value on this subject has been published in Boston, by the Rev. James Fitton. This work has been carefully and elaborately prepared, and will be read with great interest by all Catholics in America, but especially by those of New England. It is entitled *The History of the Catholic Church in New England.*

The following letter, written at the suggestion and under the supervision of the venerable Bishop of Hartford, the Right Rev. F. P. McFarland, is applicable to most of the manufacturing districts of New England. It contains the practical conclusions of one whose long residence in New England and thorough knowledge of the condition of Catholics in that part of the country give immense value to his testimony.

HARTFORD, CONN., Jan. 22, 1873.

REV. DEAR SIR:

Your note asking information concerning the resources of the Diocese of Hartford, and the prospects for emigrants, has been received, and, in answer, we would submit the following few remarks. In this diocese, which comprises the whole of the State of Connecticut, there are no "public lands" for sale. The State, which contains an area of only 4,764 square miles, is intersected by numerous railroads and streams, along which towns are springing up, whose growth is measured and interest kept alive by the location of factories in their midst and the business carried on in them.

There are several flourishing cities in the State, but their business and interests are chiefly of a manufacturing nature. The general business of the factories throughout the State consists in the manufacture of cotton and woollen goods, and articles of iron and brass at different foundries; pins, buttons, wire, tubes, axes, and clocks are also manufactured to some extent.

Foreign commerce is limited; the coasting business, however, is extensive, but chiefly with New York and New England cities. Our climate is changeable, but perhaps less so than in any other State of New England. The soil of the State is undulating, and in some portions quite rocky, but fertile. Farming interests are less encouraging than formerly, on account of the high price demanded for labor amongst "farmers' men," and "long hours."

The land in the valley of the Connecticut River is the only portion of the State now generally cultivated. The principal crops grown in this district are hay and tobacco; the latter is considered in every respect superior to any raised in this section of the country.

Mechanics command good wages, and generally find employment, if they choose to work.

Average wages for mechanics per day, $3 50; for laborers per day, $2; for girls in service per week, $3 50. Help in factories for the most part work by the "piece," and secure for themselves fair wages when business is good. Although employment is easily found by the industrious, and fair wages given for labor, still food, rents, clothing, and other ordinary necessities and comforts of life cost less in Western States. Here, it is true, all these things can be found and secured, but at a greater outlay; and for the laboring classes only where domestic economy is made a pet household virtue.

Close confinement in factories, especially in cotton and woollen mills, impairs the health of many, and those who are forced to seek employment in such places when young generally lose soon the healthy bloom and vigor of youth, and live short lives.

To Catholics of the State there is everywhere an ample opportunity of leading good Christian lives, if they wish to do so. Nearly every town and village in the State has a Catholic priest living within its limits, or is frequently visited by him. Christian instruction is therefore secured, and for this reason our people are content to build up homes for themselves and children in any portion of the diocese in which they may be found.

Assuring you that the above remarks are as complete as we could gather from our sources of information,

We remain very sincerely yours,

✠ F. P. McFarland,
per Jos. B. Reid, *Secretary*

CHAPTER II.

NEW YORK, PENNSYLVANIA, AND NEW JERSEY.

NEW YORK

LIES west of Connecticut, Massachusetts, and Vermont. It is one of the old thirteen States, and accepted the United States Constitution in July, 1788.

Area, 47,000 square miles. Population in 1870, 4,382,759; in 1860, 3,880,735. Natives of Ireland in 1870, 528,506; of Germany, 316,902.

New York has a larger population than any other State in the Union; it has also more wealth, and is consequently called the Empire State. Although emigrants are not ordinarily advised to make this State their home, still it is a settled fact that a very large number, especially of Irish emigrants, remain in New York. And when we consider the almost innumerable modes of employment in this State, the opportunities, commercial, agricultural, and otherwise, we need not be surprised that so many emigrants stay in New York. If they succeed in obtaining homes in this State, it is well that they stay in it; if not, they ought to move to some State where it can be done.

Catholic Statistics.

There are six dioceses in New York, namely: New York, Brooklyn, Albany, Ogdensburg, Rochester, and Buffalo.

The eastern part of the State is divided into the four dioceses first mentioned; the western part into the two latter. The total Catholic population of this State cannot fall short of 1,400,000.

Special statistics are as follows:

The ARCHDIOCESE OF NEW YORK comprises the city of New York, together with the counties south of the 42d degree of north latitude, excepting those on Long Island, which form the diocese of Brooklyn. There is in New York one archbishop, whose province embraces New England, New York, and New Jersey; two hundred and forty-one priests, and sixty-seven clerical students; one hundred and twenty-eight churches, and twenty-four chapels; one ecclesiastical seminary, and three colleges; eight religious communities of men, and twelve of women. Schools and academies in the same proportion. The Catholic population may be estimated at 600,000.

The DIOCESE OF BROOKLYN, comprising all of Long Island, and established in 1853, has one bishop, residing in Brooklyn; one hundred and two priests, and a large number of clerical students; about eighty churches and chapels, one college, and a great number of schools, parochial and select. The Catholic population is at least 200,000.

The DIOCESE OF ALBANY, established in 1847, has one bishop and one coadjutor-bishop, residing at Albany; one hundred and twenty priests, and thirty clerical students; one hundred and seventy churches and chapels, and one hundred stations; a large supply of academies, select and parochial schools. Catholic population, over 200,000.

The DIOCESE OF OGDENSBURG, established in 1872, comprises the northeastern part of New York, and has one bishop, residing in Ogdensburg; forty-two priests, and ten clerical students; sixty-five churches and chapels, and thirty-eight stations. Catholic population, about 50,000.

The DIOCESE OF ROCHESTER, established in 1868, comprises the counties of the central portion of the State lying between the dioceses of Albany on the east, and of Buffalo on the west. This diocese has one bishop, residing in Rochester; forty-seven priests, and thirty-one clerical students; sixty-four churches. Catholic population, about 60,000.

The DIOCESE OF BUFFALO, established in 1847, comprises the western part of New York, and has one bishop, residing in Buffalo; one hundred and thirteen priests, and eighteen clerical students; one hundred and eighteen churches and chapels, and eight churches building. The Catholic population is probably 200,000.

It is interesting to Catholics to know that the first church in what is now the great State of New York was built on the site of the present St. Peter's, corner of Barclay and Church Streets, in 1786. Its dimensions were eighty-one feet in length by forty-eight in width. It was erected mainly by the exertions of the Rev. William O'Brian, a Dominican priest from Ireland, who raised most of the funds necessary in Mexico and Cuba. This church, showing signs of decay, and, besides, being too small for the congregation, was taken down in 1836 to give place to the present massive structure of the same name. The first Mass was said in it on the 4th of November, 1786, and the last on the 28th of August, 1836, having thus been used nearly fifty years.

The *History of the Catholic Church in New York*, by Archbishop Bayley, is highly interesting, and ought to be in every Catholic library.

PENNSYLVANIA

lies south of New York, and west of New Jersey. This is also one of the old thirteen States, and accepted the Constitution of the United States in December, 1787. Area (almost the same as that of New York), forty-six thousand square miles. Population in 1870, 3,521,791; in 1860, 2,906,215. Natives of Ireland in 1870, 235,-750; of Germany, 60,145.

The prospects for emigrants in this State are very much the same as in New York. In neither State can they be compared with the opportunities of making independent homes in the States of the South or of the far West. A very great variety of employment is presented to industrious men in this State; and no one need be idle if he is willing to work at fair wages. The land is generally in price beyond the reach of most emigrants, ranging from twenty to three hundred dollars per acre. Very little land, however, can be purchased at the former price.

In northeastern Pennsylvania, the coal-beds are said

to be the most extensive in the world; in the west, also, they are successfully worked. Iron ore abounds in nearly the whole State, and Pennsylvania takes the lead of all the States in iron manufactures of all kinds. About one-half of all the iron produced in the United States is found in this State.

Catholic Statistics in 1873.

There are five dioceses in this State, of which Phila delphia, Harrisburg, and Pittsburg occupy the southern portion, whilst Erie takes up the northwestern and Scranton the northeastern parts of the State. The Catholic population does not fall short of 550,000 souls. There were many Catholics in this State previous to the American Revolution; and the celebrated brigade, known in those days as the "Pennsylvania Line," was almost entirely made up of Irish Catholics. The first Commodore of the American navy, John Barry, an Irish Catholic, made this State his home, and died in Philadelphia in 1803. Thomas Fitzsimon is also honorably mentioned.

The Diocese of Philadelphia established in 1808, comprises the city of Philadelphia and nine counties in the southeastern part of the State. It has one bishop, living in Philadelphia; two hundred and two priests, and one hundred and five clerical students; one hundred and seven churches, thirty-six chapels, and thirty-three stations. This diocese is admirably supplied with colleges, academies, schools, and Catholic institutions of all kinds. Catholic population, about 250,000.

The Diocese of Harrisburg, established in 1868, comprises the counties west of the diocese of Philadelphia, and east of those of Pittsburg. It has one bishop, residing in Harrisburg; thirty-three priests, and seventeen clerical students; forty-nine churches, and twenty-two chapels and stations. Catholic population, probably 40,000.

The Diocese of Pittsburg, established in 1843, comprises the city of Pittsburg and the counties of the southwestern part of the State. It has one bishop, living in Pittsburg; one hundred and forty-three priests, and thirty-five clerical students; one hundred and nineteen churches, and fifteen chapels. The supply of Catholic institutions of all kinds is very large in this diocese. Catholic population, about 150,000.

The Diocese of Erie, established in 1853, comprises the northwestern counties of the State, and has one bishop, residing at Erie; fifty-two priests, and twelve clerical students; sixty churches; and a Catholic population of 40,000.

The following letter is from the Rev. Thos. A. Casey, Secretary of the Right Rev. Bishop Mullen, of Erie. Though brief, it is a valuable contribution to the present work, inasmuch as it gives practical and reliable information on the subject of which it treats:

St. Patrick's Cathedral, Erie, Feb. 5, 1873.

Very Rev. Father Byrne:

Dear Sir: Your letter to Bishop Mullen, requiring information concerning price of land, wages, etc., has been handed me, with request to answer. The counties of which this diocese is made up are, as a general thing, very rough. Land is not very high in price, save along the lake shore. Land, I dare say, in some of the interior counties, might be purchased for $10 per acre; while along the lake it runs up as high as $150, or even higher. The great oil region is in this diocese, and that alone gives employment to a great number of men, so that wages, as a general thing, are always good. In summer men can make even five or six dollars per day, and in winter probably nearly one-half that, provided they are not worthless.

I am yours sincerely,

THOS. A. CASEY.

The DIOCESE OF SCRANTON, established in 1868, comprises the counties of northeastern Pennsylvania. It has one bishop, living in Scranton; thirty-eight priests, and fifteen clerical students; sixty-two churches, and forty-one stations. Catholic population, probably 50,000.

The following letter is from a very reliable source, and gives a plain, honest statement of the prospects for emigrants in northeastern Pennsylvania, which constitutes the diocese of Scranton:

FEBRUARY 10, 1873.

REV. S. BYRNE:

DEAR SIR: In reply to your request, I may inform you that the Diocese of Scranton embraces ten counties in the northeastern part of Pennsylvania, as may be seen in the *Catholic Directory*. The only county of importance is Luzerne. The other counties are not remarkable for good quality of land; there is here and there good farming, but, comparing this section with the other parts of Pennsylvania, there is a marked difference. In general, it is hilly and rocky. There is very little inducement for settlers to locate here. In Luzerne, there are rolling-mills and machine-shops, and mining is carried on very extensively. A machinist makes $3 per day; a laborer about $2. In the rolling-mill, a puddler, $4; a helper, $2; a miner on an average, $3 50; a laborer, $2.

NEW JERSEY

lies south of New York and east of Pennsylvania. Area, 8,320 square miles. Population in 1870, 906,096; in 1860, 672,085. Natives of Ireland in 1870, 86,734; of Germany, 54,000. This is also one of the original States, and ratified the Constitution in January, 1788.

New Jersey, lying between the two great cities of New York and Philadelphia, has many advantages in the way of supplying the markets of these cities with vegetables and fruits. Gardening, therefore, and fruit-growing are the principal sources of wealth in this State. Manufacturing is also very extensively carried on in Newark, Paterson, and other cities. New Jersey is becoming densely populated by the business and working classes of the neighboring cities, the railroad companies of the State giving all manner of facilities to mechanics and business men for reaching their places of occupation at a convenient hour. Around the different railroad stations towns and villages are growing up, and there is every chance for small capitalists to obtain homes almost anywhere in this State.

The DIOCESE OF NEWARK, established in 1853, comprises the whole State of New Jersey, and has one bishop, living at Newark; ninety-three priests, and several clerical students. Catholic population, about 250,000.

CHAPTER III.

MARYLAND, DELAWARE, VIRGINIA, WEST VIRGINIA.

MARYLAND,

LYING west of Delaware, and south of Pennsylvania, is the cradle-land of English-speaking Catholics in the United States. The first colony, under George Calvert, Lord Baltimore, in 1633, was a Catholic colony. Maryland is also one of the original States of the Union, having ratified the Constitution of the United States in 1788. Area, 9,356 square miles. Population in 1870, 781,000; in 1860, 687,000. Natives of Ireland in 1870, 23,630; of Germany, 47,045.

The climate of Maryland is temperate and healthy, except on the lowlands bordering the Chesapeake Bay. The principal article of export is tobacco, which is cultivated with great success in this State. Other species of industry, such as the manufacture of cotton, wool, iron, and flour, flourish also. The price of land ranges from $5 to $150 an acre. Very little land, however, can be bought at the first-named price, and it is seldom we find it as high as $150. The average price is about $40 an acre. Oyster-dredging is one of the features of this State, and, according to the census returns of 1870, employs about ten thousand men.

THE DISTRICT OF COLUMBIA,

formerly a part of Maryland, and situated on the Potomac River, is the seat of Government of the United States. It was selected by Washington for this purpose towards the close of the last century, Philadelphia having been previously the seat of the general Government. Area, 60 square miles. Population in 1870, 131,700; in 1860, 75,080. Natives of Ireland in 1870, 8,218; of Germany, 4,920.

The principal employment in Washington is connected with the various departments of Government, and these furnish employment to great numbers, but more especially to copyists, printers, book-binders, and clerks of all kinds.

Catholic Statistics in 1873.

The ARCHDIOCESE OF BALTIMORE, which comprises all of the State of Maryland west of the Chesapeake, and the District of Columbia, is the oldest diocese in the United States, having been established in the year 1790, as already mentioned. It has one archbishop, residing in Baltimore, who is the Metropolitan of the church in the United States; one hundred and ninety-five priests, and one hundred and twenty-five churches; thirty-five chapels and stations, and a very large number of religious institutions, both male and female, all in a most flourishing condition.. Catholic population, probably 250,000.

Some of the most distinguished men of the United States have been Catholics of Maryland. Among these may be mentioned Charles Carroll of Carrollton, who outlived all his companions that signed the Declaration of Independence of the United States; and, in more recent times, Judge Taney, who was Chief-Justice of the United States over thirty years.

DELAWARE,

lying south of Pennsylvania and east of Maryland, is another of the old thirteen States, and accepted the Constitution of the United States in December, 1787. Excepting Rhode Island, it is the smallest State in the Union, the area being only 2,120 square miles.

Population in 1870, 125,015; in 1860, 112,216. Natives of Ireland in 1870, 6,000; of Germany, 1,142.

Agriculture is the principal occupation of the people of Delaware; but at Wilmington, the principal city, manufacturing, especially that of gunpowder, is extensively carried on. Ship-building is also a specialty of this city.

The Diocese of Wilmington, established in 1868, comprises all of Delaware and that part of Maryland and Virginia which lies east of the Chesapeake Bay. The statistics for 1873 are as follows: one bishop, residing at Wilmington; sixteen priests, and four clerical students. Catholic population, about 15,000.

VIRGINIA

is one of the oldest States in the Union, the first settlement on the James River having been made in 1612. Virginia took a most important part in the war of Independence, furnishing some of the most distinguished patriots—such as Washington, Henry, Jefferson, Madison, and Monroe—in that grand struggle for human freedom. Virginia received the Constitution of the United States in July, 1788.

This State lies southwest of Maryland, and has an area of 41,352 square miles. Population in 1870, 1,225,163; in 1860, 1,219,630. Natives of Ireland in 1870, 5,191; of Germany, 4,050.

The climate of Virginia is salubrious and beautiful; the soil, especially in the river valleys, is most productive; and, taken all in all, this State presents as many attractions to the honest and industrious emigrant as any State in the Union. All kinds of grain are raised in abundance; but tobacco is the great article of export. Manufacturing is extensively carried on, especially in Richmond, the capital of the State, where we find fifty tobacco factories.

Good land can be had in almost every county of this State, from $2 to $30 an acre. The system of labor and industry having been disturbed by the late Civil War, there is a cordial welcome extended to foreigners of all nationalities who avoid politics as a *trade*, and betake themselves to any industrial pursuit. The population of this State may be doubled or trebled with advantage to all concerned.

Catholic Statistics in 1873.

The DIOCESE OF RICHMOND, established in 1821, comprises all of the State, excepting five counties in the west, which belong to the Diocese of Wheeling. It has one bishop, residing at Richmond; twenty-one priests, and eleven clerical students; fifteen churches, and eighteen chapels and stations; several religious institutions and schools; and a Catholic population of nearly 20,000.

WEST VIRGINIA,

lying south of Pennsylvania and west of Virginia, is a new State, having been formed out of the territory of Virginia and admitted as a State in 1863. Area, 20,000 square miles. Population in 1870, 442,014; in 1860, 377,000. Natives of Ireland in 1870, 6,832; of Germany, 6,232.

This is a very mountainous State, especially the eastern part of it; the soil is good, however, and the climate very healthy. Land may be had in almost every part of this State at prices ranging from $1 to $20 an acre, and on long time. I have before me the *West Virginia Hand-Book and Immigrant's Guide*, by J. H. D. Debar—a work of great value, and very reliable in its account of the agricultural, mineral, and manufacturing interests of the State. It may be had by application in writing or otherwise to Gibbons Bros., Printers, Parkersburg, W. Va.

The DIOCESE OF WHEELING, established in 1850, comprises the whole State of West Virginia and five counties of Virginia. It has one bishop, living at Wheeling; twenty-nine priests, and fourteen clerical students; forty-eight churches, seven chapels, and forty stations; institutions in proportion. Catholic population, about 20,000.

CHAPTER IV.

NORTH CAROLINA, SOUTH CAROLINA, GEORGIA, FLORIDA.

NORTH CAROLINA

LIES south of Virginia, having the Atlantic Ocean as its eastern boundary. It is one of the original States of the Union, and accepted the United States Constitution in May, 1790. Area, 45,000 square miles. Population in 1870, 1,071,361; in 1860, 992,622. Natives of Ireland in 1870, 677; of Germany, 904.

The western part of this State is mountainous; the Alleghanies, running southwestwardly through Pennsylvania and Virginia, reach their highest elevation (6,775 feet) here. To emigrants the following extract, taken from the *United States Catholic Almanac* of 1873, will be useful: "North Carolina holds out many inducements to emigrants whose object is to devote themselves to agricultural pursuits. In the western and northern portions of the State particularly, the climate is mild and salubrious, and the soil well adapted for grain and cotton crops. Land can be purchased at prices varying from fifty cents to ten dollars an acre. Catholics are advised to select lands contiguous to churches, where they may enjoy the ministrations of their holy religion."

One of the most distinguished jurists of the United States, Judge Gaston, was a native of this State, and a fervent Catholic.

The VICARIATE APOSTOLIC OF NORTH CAROLINA, as it is known in the Catholic Church, comprises the whole State of North Carolina, and has one vicar apostolic, residing in Wilmington; eight priests, and seven clerical students; ten churches and chapels, and twenty stations. Catholic population, about 1,500.

SOUTH CAROLINA

lies south of North Carolina, and west of the Atlantic Ocean. Originally the two Carolinas formed one colony; but they were divided in 1729. This is one of the original thirteen States, and ratified the Constitution in June, 1788. Area, 24,500 square miles. Population in 1870, 705,606; in 1860, 703,708. Natives of Ireland in 1870, 3,262; of Germany, 2,761.

This State suffered immensely in the late Civil War, the principal cities having been laid in ruins. This accounts for the very slight increase in the population. The climate is hot and unhealthy for Europeans in the low or marshy lands; in the hilly regions, it is beautiful and healthy. Many of the towns in the interior, such as Aiken, are sought for by invalids in the winter season on account of their great salubrity. Cotton is the great staple of this State; but agriculture of all kinds may be successfully engaged in. Good land near railroads can be purchased for two dollars an acre; and very little land for sale goes beyond five dollars. There is every opportunity in this State for Europeans to obtain homes as cheap and as healthy as in any part of the United States.

The DIOCESE OF CHARLESTON, established in 1820, with the renowned Bishop England as its first bishop, comprises the whole State of South Carolina, and also the Bahama Islands. It has one bishop, residing at Charleston; fifteen priests; and several flourishing religious institutions. Catholic population not given.

GEORGIA

lies south of North and South Carolina and Tennessee. It is one of the old States, and accepted the Constitution in January, 1788. Area, 58,000 square miles. Population in 1870, 1,184,000; in 1860, 1,057,286. Natives of Ireland in 1870, 5,093; of Germany, 2,761.

Georgia was originally settled by English Methodists and Scotch Highlanders; but, in the lapse of years, the character of the population has greatly changed.

The principal productions are cotton, rice, Indian corn, and sweet potatoes. Iron and coal are abundant. Lumber of a superior quality is one of the staples of this State. Manufacturing is extensive, and increases every year.

Unimproved land may be bought in every part of Georgia for one dollar an acre, and sometimes for less; improved lands range in price from $3 to $20 an acre. Land in the near neighborhood of cities and towns may be bought for the last-named price. The following letter is from an intelligent correspondent of the United States Bureau of Statistics for 1870:

"I believe there are better chances for persons who wish to farm on a small scale in middle Georgia than in any other part of the country; for, if they have no capital, they can rent land for one-half the products, and have everything furnished. I can cite instances where poor men by farming in that manner saved enough in a year to buy the places they worked. The climate, soil, scarcity of labor, and cheapness of land make this the most desirable place for immigration in the world.

"Where emigrants in the Northwest would have to wait several years to derive any profit from their labor, they can here reap large profits at once; for the land is ready for the seed, the markets are near, and the principal staple always commands a good price."

The DIOCESE OF SAVANNAH, established in 1850, comprises the State of Georgia. It has (1873) one bishop, residing in Savannah; twelve priests, and five clerical students; twelve churches built, and six building; thirty chapels and stations; a fair supply of religious institutions of all kinds, and a Catholic population of 20,000.

The following is from the *Catholic Almanac* of 1873:

"The soil and climate invite settlers to come here and work to their own advantage the agricultural resources of the State, and these are inexhaustible. Catholics are not advised to settle in sectarian districts, where they and their children would be exposed to the danger of a shipwreck of their holy faith. But if they understand gardening (even slightly), and have a small capital, they will find in the vicinity of cities rich lots, the cultivation of which will amply repay their industry."

FLORIDA

lies south of Georgia and Alabama, and was admitted as a State of the Union in 1845. The oldest settlement within the present limits of the United States was made at St. Augustine. The Catholic church of that place was built in 1570; the first martyr of Catholic truth in the United States was the Dominican, Father Louis Cancer de Barbastro, who was killed here by the Indians on the 26th of June, 1547.

Area of Florida, 59,000 square miles. Population in 1870, 188,000; in 1860, 140,104. Natives of Ireland in 1870, 737; of Germany, 597.

In the *Catholic Almanac* of 1873 we read as follows: "Catholic gardeners and farmers who would like a pleasant place to settle in would do well to try the vicinity of St. Augustine. The place was originally settled by Catholics; and the Catholic element largely prevails there to this day. The cultivation of the vine is carried on with great success all over the State." Florida is a favorite resort for invalids, especially consumptives, in the winter season.

St. Augustine, erected into a vicariate apostolic in 1857, and into an episcopal see in 1870, comprises all of Florida, excepting a few counties in the western part of the State. There is one bishop, living at St. Augustine, twelve priests, nineteen churches and chapels, and seventy stations where Mass is said. Catholic population, 10,000.

CHAPTER V.

TENNESSEE, ALABAMA, MISSISSIPPI, LOUISIANA, TEXAS, ARKANSAS.

TENNESSEE

LIES directly west of North Carolina, and north of Mississippi and Alabama. It is an old State, having been admitted into the Union in June, 1796. Area, 45,000 square miles. Population in 1870, 1,258,000; in 1860, 1,109,081. Natives of Ireland in 1870, 8,044; of Germany, 4,539.

Tennessee is ordinarily divided into three parts—Eastern, Middle, and Western. The climate of Eastern and Middle Tennessee is unsurpassed for mildness and salubrity. The river valleys in the western part are most fertile, but not healthy.

In nearly all the counties of this State, improved (or cleared) land may be bought for prices ranging from $3 to $20 an acre; unimproved land may be bought from $1 to $10. Tennessee is well supplied with railroads, and is likely to become, in a few years, a prosperous and wealthy State. A paper entitled the *Rural Sun*, published in Nashville, is exclusively devoted to the object of making known the agricultural, mineral, and manufacturing resources of the State; and makes it a specialty to give most valuable and correct information to all wishing to settle in this part of the country. Europeans of all nationalities receive a cordial welcome in this State; as, indeed, they receive in all States of the West and South. I am indebted to Messrs. Donohoe, Bulkley & Co., of Memphis, Tennessee, for valuable documents. These gentlemen will furnish the most reliable information to those desiring it.

The CATHOLIC DIOCESE OF NASHVILLE, established in 1837, comprises the whole State of Tennessee, and has one bishop, residing in Nashville; twenty-seven priests, and twenty-five churches. Nashville and Memphis, the principal cities of the State, are well supplied with religious institutions of all kinds. Catholic population, probably 20,000.

ALABAMA

lies west of Georgia, and has Florida and the Gulf of Mexico for its southern boundary. Area, 50,700 square miles. Population in 1870, 997,000; in 1860, 964,201. Natives of Ireland in 1870, 4,000; of Germany, 2,500.

Alabama was admitted as a State in December, 1819. It is the greatest cotton-growing State in the Union. It is also adapted for all other kinds of agriculture. Northern Alabama is especially congenial to Europeans, and good land is cheap in all parts of the State. Small, improved farms may be purchased for sums ranging between $3 and $20 an acre; unimproved land may be had from 50 cents to $10 an acre. Manufacturing is on the increase; and the disastrous effects of the late Civil War will, it is hoped, soon cease to be felt in this State. Irish and German emigrants are received with a hearty welcome.

The DIOCESE OF MOBILE, established in 1824, comprises the whole State of Alabama and the western part of Florida. It has one bishop, living in Mobile, thirty-three priests, and eight clerical students; twenty-eight churches, and a good supply of religious institutions. Catholic population, about 14,000.

MISSISSIPPI

lies west of Alabama, and has the river Mississippi, the "Father of Waters," as its western boundary. This State was admitted into the Union in December, 1817. Area, 47,200 square miles. Population in 1870, 828,-000; in 1860, 791,305. Natives of Ireland in 1870, 3,500; of Germany, about 2,300.

Mississippi holds out the greatest inducements to industrious white people from all parts of the world. I say *white* people, because the colored people* are no longer reliable as farm laborers. The southeastern part of the State is almost entirely Government land, and offers to actual settlers all the advantages attaching to such lands in all parts of the country. Improved farms may be bought in all other parts of the State in quantities reaching from twenty to one thousand acres, at prices ranging from $2 to $25 an acre. Unimproved land may be bought at from $1 to $10, according to location, soil, etc. In this State, as in Alabama and other Southern States, several crops of certain kinds can be raised on the same land every year. "Vegetables and fruits ripen six or eight weeks earlier than they do north

* Negroes.

of the Ohio River; and several railroads, besides the great river, which is always open for navigation, give cheap and quick transportation to the markets of the Northern and Eastern States."—*Catholic Almanac*, 1873.

The DIOCESE OF NATCHEZ, established in 1837, comprises the whole State of Mississippi. It has one bishop, residing at Natchez; twenty-six priests, and seven clerical students; twenty-eight churches built, and three building. Catholic population not given, but probably 15,000.

LOUISIANA

lies west of Mississippi; was purchased from the French in 1803, and became a State in April, 1812. The original settlements, dating back to the close of the seventeenth century, were made by the French. The French language is still spoken by a large part of the population. Area, 46,500 square miles. Population in 1870, 726,915; in 1860, 708,000. Natives of Ireland in 1870, 17,068; of Germany, 19,000.

In regard to the prospects for emigrants in this State, what has been already specified regarding the neighboring States may, in general, be applied to this. The land is about the same in price; but, generally speaking, it cannot be purchased except in large farms.

Catholic Statistics in 1873.

This is an old Catholic settlement, and there are two dioceses in the State—the Archdiocese of New Orleans, and the Diocese of Natchitoches.

The ARCHDIOCESE OF NEW ORLEANS, established in

1793, comprises the southern part of the State. It has one archbishop, residing in New Orleans; one hundred and fifty-nine priests, and forty-five clerical students; ninety-two churches, and twenty-seven chapels and stations. There is a large number of religious and literary institutions of all kinds. Catholic population not given, but probably amounts to over 200,000.

The DIOCESE OF NATCHITOCHES, established in 1857, comprises the northern part of the State. It has one bishop, living at Natchitoches; twenty-nine priests, and two clerical students; twenty-six churches and chapels. Catholic population, about 24,000.

TEXAS

lies west of Louisiana and Arkansas, and is the largest State of the Union. Its area is 237,000 square miles, being seven times as large as Ireland, and nearly five times as large as New York. It was admitted into the Union in December, 1845. Population in 1870, 819,-000; in 1860, 756,168. Natives of Ireland in 1870, 4,031; of Germany, 24,000.

In regard to the prospects of emigrants in this State, it is well to remark that in so vast a territory all varieties of soil and climate may be looked for. Western Texas is remarkable as being probably the greatest grazing country in the world. The immense herds are fed on natural pastures.* The soil in general is extremely fertile.

* We read in Dr. Latham's work, *Trans-Missouri Stock-raising*, page 54, that one of the most extensive cattle-raisers in all Texas is Mr. Thomas O'Connor, of the San Antonio valley. He is a native of Wexford, Ireland. He had forty thousand cattle in 1862.

Land may be purchased in any part of Texas for sums ranging from 25 cents (a British shilling) to $10 or $15 an acre. It is expected that, in a few years, the Southern Pacific Railroad will pass through Texas, and this will give a great impetus to all kinds of industrial pursuits. The chances for emigrants are very favorable.

The DIOCESE OF GALVESTON, established in 1847, comprises the whole State of Texas. It has one bishop, residing in Galveston; eighty-three priests, and five clerical students; fifty-five churches and chapels. Catholic population, about 180,000.

ARKANSAS

lies directly north of Louisiana, and west of the river Mississippi. It was first settled by the French, and made a part of Louisiana. It became a State in June, 1836. Area, 52,000 square miles. Population in 1870, 484,000; in 1860, 435,450. Natives of Ireland in 1870, 1,428; of Germany, 1,567.

The soil of Arkansas, especially of the eastern part, is exceedingly fertile. At least twenty counties of the State are admirably adapted for growing cotton. The crop is usually most abundant, and enables men who raise it to pay for their land in one or two years. The other parts of the State are hilly or rolling; and all kinds of agriculture may be profitably engaged in. Land from one to twenty dollars an acre.

The following letter, from a highly respected and reliable source, will be read with interest. It contains in a brief form some valuable suggestions:

"LITTLE ROCK, ARK., March 2, 1873.

"REV. AND DEAR FRIEND: All I can do at present is to give you some general views on the subject of your letter. First, I think all our cities are overcrowded with poor.

"Secondly, the natural outlet is the country.

"Thirdly, experience shows that, if they migrate singly, except it be to Catholic colonies, they are lost in the general non-Catholic community—they lose the faith, and allow their children to grow up without a knowledge of the faith.

"Fourthly, the plan to pursue, therefore, is concerted migration.

"Fifthly, I think this Southern country offers more inducements to emigrants in the advantages of soil, climate, and cheapness of land than the Northern States. As you are aware, the South has its drawbacks also, such as corrupt governments (in some few States), high taxes, and malarious diseases, especially in the river valleys. But these will soon disappear; and it is well to bear in mind that the whole country is becoming covered with a network of railroads."

The DIOCESE OF LITTLE ROCK, established in 1843, comprises the whole State of Arkansas and the Indian Territory west of it. It has (1873) one bishop, residing in Little Rock; ten priests, and two clerical students; eighteen churches, and twenty-five stations. Catholic population, about 2,500.

The following is from the *Catholic Almanac* for 1873:

"The diocese of Little Rock has about four thousand acres of land, which it would sell on very easy terms to a Catholic colony. We do not recommend individual families to purchase, as it would be very difficult for a scattered few to have the ministrations of a clergyman."

For particulars address, Very Rev. P. O'Reilly, V.G., Little Rock.

CHAPTER VI.

KENTUCKY, OHIO, INDIANA, AND MICHIGAN.

KENTUCKY

LIES north of Tennessee and west of Virginia. It is an old State, having been received into the Union in June, 1792. Area, 37,700 square miles. Population in 1870, 1,321,000; in 1860, 1,156,000. Natives of Ireland in 1870, 22,000; of Germany, 30,000.

Kentucky is a rich and prosperous State; land cannot be bought for anything like so low a price as in the States through which we have been advancing. Improved land is held at from twenty to one hundred dollars an acre, and unimproved land from five to thirty dollars. There is demand for labor, especially agricultural, in all parts of the State. The climate is generally very healthy, and the soil excellent. Indian corn, wheat, and tobacco are raised in great abundance. The Ohio River forms the northern boundary of the State, and, together with the Mississippi on the west, and several railroads, furnishes large facilities for trade.

There are two Catholic dioceses in Kentucky—that of Louisville, and that of Covington.

The DIOCESE OF LOUISVILLE (formerly of Bardstown, established in 1808), comprises the western part of Kentucky, and is one of the oldest dioceses in the United States. It has one bishop, residing in Louisville; ninety-eight priests, and thirty clerical students; eighty churches and several stations. It is extraordinarily well supplied with religious institutions of all kinds, but especially with academies of a high order of excellence. Catholic population, 100,000.*

The DIOCESE OF COVINGTON, established in 1853, comprises the eastern part of the State, and has (1873) one bishop, residing in Covington; forty-two priests, and eighteen clerical students; forty-five churches, and forty-five chapels and stations; several religious institutions. Catholic population, 30,000.

OHIO

lies north of Kentucky and west of Pennsylvania. It was received into the Union as a State in June, 1802. Area, 40,000 square miles. Population in 1870, 2,665,200; in 1860, 2,329,511. Natives of Ireland in 1870, 82,764; of Germany, 183,000.

Ohio is a magnificent State, whether viewed in regard to her agricultural, mineral, or manufacturing resources. Smaller than New York and Pennsylvania, she comes next to them in population. Land is rather higher in price than in Kentucky, ranging from twenty-five to two hundred dollars an acre. Labor of all kinds is in great demand, however, in all parts of the State. In the southeastern part, immense beds of coal and iron are being opened up; and persons having any experience in mining are consequently in great demand. Skilled labor of all kinds is certain to meet a market and good remuneration almost anywhere in this State.

* The *Sketches of Kentucky*, by Bishop Spalding, is highly interesting.

Catholic Statistics in 1873.

There are three dioceses in this State: the Archdiocese of Cincinnati, and the Dioceses of Columbus and Cleveland. The aggregate Catholic population of the State amounts to 400,000.

The ARCHDIOCESE OF CINCINNATI, established in 1822, comprises the southwestern part of the State. It has, in 1873, one archbishop, residing in Cincinnati; one hundred and forty-three priests, and forty-five clerical students; one hundred and eighty-five churches built, and nine building; eighteen chapels, and sixty stations. There is a large number of religious institutions. Catholic population, 220,000.

The DIOCESE OF COLUMBUS, established in 1868, comprises the southeastern part of the State, and has one bishop, living at Columbus; forty-six priests, and twenty-two clerical students; fifty-two churches, and twenty-three chapels and stations. It is well supplied with religious institutions. Catholic population, about 60,000.

The great coal and iron region of Ohio lies almost entirely within this diocese; and this fact alone is likely to attract a large population.

The DIOCESE OF CLEVELAND, established in 1847, comprises the northern part of Ohio, and has one bishop, living in Cleveland; one hundred and thirty-three priests, and sixty clerical students; one hundred and sixty-five churches built, and twelve building. Catholic population, 120,000.

INDIANA

lies west of Ohio, and north of Kentucky. Area, 33,-809 square miles. Population in 1870, 1,681,000; in 1860, 1,350,428. Natives of Ireland in 1870, 29,000; of Germany, 78,000.

Indiana was admitted into the Union in December, 1816. The first settlement was at Vincennes, where a small French colony was established in the beginning of the last century.

The remarks already made respecting Ohio apply generally to Indiana. It is a very prosperous State. The climate is good, and the soil excellent. Indian corn and wheat are the great staples. The coal-beds of this State are quite extensive, and afford remunerative employment to large numbers. Improved land may be bought in a few places as low as $4 an acre; but generally it ranges from $15 to $150. Unimproved land may be bought as low as $2 an acre, ranging from that to $40. There is demand for all kinds of labor, skilled and unskilled.

There are two Catholic dioceses in this State—of Vincennes, namely, and Fort Wayne. Catholic population of the whole State, about 120,000.

The Diocese of Vincennes, established in 1834, comprises the southern part of the State. It has one bishop, residing at Vincennes; ninety-six priests, and thirty clerical students; one hundred and thirty-six churches, and twelve chapels, besides seventy stations. Catholic institutions are numerous. Catholic population, about 80,000.

The DIOCESE OF FORT WAYNE, established in 1857, comprises northern Indiana, and has one bishop, living in Fort Wayne; sixty-nine priests, and five clerical students; seventy-seven churches built, and seven building; fourteen chapels. Catholic population not given, but probably amounts to 40,000.

MICHIGAN

lies directly north of Ohio and Indiana. It was first settled by the French, and was admitted as a State in January, 1837. Area, 56,250 square miles. Population in 1870, 1,184,109; in 1860, 749,113. Natives of Ireland in 1870, 42,013; of Germany, 64,103. There are also 35,000 English.

The following extracts from the Report of the Commissioner of the State Land Office at Lansing will be read with interest by all:

MICHIGAN STATE LAND OFFICE,
LANSING, October 1, 1872.

To His Excellency HENRY P. BALDWIN,
Governor of the State of Michigan:

SIR: In compliance with the provisions of law governing this department, I have the honor to present the following report for the fiscal year ending September 30, 1872:

STATE LANDS.—HISTORIC OUTLINE.

Michigan originally formed part of the region ceded to the United States by the State of Virginia, described as the "Territory northwest of the Ohio." The cession embraced the country now within the limits of Ohio, Indiana, Illinois, Michigan, Wisconsin, and the eastern part of Minnesota, having an aggregate area of 213,000 square miles. Michigan was first erected into a Territory by the act of January 11, 1805, and admitted as a State by act of January 26, 1837. It is separated on the north and east from the Dominion of Canada by Lake Superior, River St. Marie, Lake Huron, St. Clair River, Lake St. Clair, and Detroit River, having Ohio and Indiana on the south, and Lake Michigan and the State of Wisconsin on the west, embracing an area of 56,451 square miles, or 36,128,640 acres. The State is divided into two peninsulas, northern and southern, separated by the Straits of Mackinaw, uniting Lakes Huron and Michigan.

"The Northern Peninsula" in its greatest length is 316 miles, and from 30 to 120 wide, embracing two-fifths of the whole area of the State, or 22,580 square miles. This peninsula presents a striking contrast in soil and surface to the southern; the latter being generally level or undulating, and very fertile, the former rugged, and in certain portions even mountainous, the streams abounding in rapids and waterfalls, rendering the scenery very picturesque and beautiful. The climate of the Northern Peninsula is rigorous, and the soil sterile, fully compensated, however, by the extensive deposits of copper and iron.* The eastern portion is less rugged than the western, where mountains attain an altitude of nearly 2,000 feet.

The central portion of this peninsula is rolling table-land, for the most part timbered with white-pine, spruce, hemlock, birch, oak, aspen, maple, ash, and elm; abounding in rich deposits of copper, extending from Keweenaw Point, on Lake Superior, to the western borders of the State. Minerals also exist on Isle Royale, which embraces an area of 230 square miles. These localities, together with Ontonagon and Portage Lake, constitute the principal mining regions.

The vast deposits of iron ore in Marquette County are apparently inexhaustible, and the ore produces the best iron to be found in the world. There are also reports of the recent dis-

* There are many Irish people in this part of the State.

covery of valuable deposits of silver near the southern shore of Lake Superior, in township 51 north, range 42 west, and it is not within the province of reasonable conjecture to compute the wealth that lies entombed in the caverns and hidden by the rocks and hills of the Northern Peninsula of Michigan, whose northern shore is washed by the bright and sparkling waters of Lake Superior, the largest expanse of fresh water on the globe, embracing an area of 23,000 square miles, with a coast line of 1,500 miles.

The Southern Peninsula includes three-fifths of the entire area of the State, being 275 miles from north to south, and 175 miles on the southern boundary from Lake Erie to Lake Michigan, its greatest width being 200 miles, between Lakes Huron and Michigan. This peninsula, so interesting in its agricultural and economical aspects, has the greater portion of the population and improvements. It is generally level, rising gradually from the Lakes on the east and west to a vast undulating plain in the interior, covered for the most part with various kinds of oak, black-walnut, sugar-maple, elm, linden, hickory, ash, basswood, locust, dogwood, poplar, beech, aspen, chestnut, cedar, tamarack, and paw-paw, while pine is found in great abundance in nearly all parts of the northern half of the peninsula. A small portion of the area is prairie. A considerable portion, however, is termed "oak openings," which are beautiful and fertile natural lawns, dotted over with scattering trees, and free from undergrowth. The great fertility of the soil is everywhere attested by a luxuriant flora, and by crops of cereals, fruits, and vegetables.

The wheat yield of Michigan is not surpassed by that of any other State in the Union, taking into account the quantity and quality of the production. Indian corn, rye, oats, barley, buckwheat, and potatoes are also cultivated extensively, while sheep, horses, cattle, and swine are receiving marked attention.

Southern Michigan has already become one of the greatest apple-growing regions of the Union. Peaches are raised successfully in the region bordering on Lake Michigan as far north as Grand Traverse Bay, while pears, plums, cherries, quinces, and all the different varieties of small fruits are grown throughout the State. Along the shore of Lake Michigan, in the valleys of the St. Joseph, Grand, Kalamazoo, and Detroit Rivers, including the islands, as well as on the shore of Lake Erie, vine culture has given proof that these localities are well adapted to the grape, while the more hardy varieties may be successfully grown in the interior portions of the State, and past results from this branch of industry give promise of great increase.

Wool-growing is a leading agricultural interest, and coal and salt occupy a prominent position in our material resources; but the lumber trade is a most important interest, giving employment to millions of dollars of capital and to thousands of the hearty and robust sons of toil, whose sinewy arms are converting our extensive forests of pine and other timber into the necessary material for the construction of cottages for the poor and palaces for the more favored class.

In addition to our *material* resources, the State abounds in a variety of scenery, on which the gaze of the pleasure-seeking tourist, the calm contemplation of the philosopher, the wearied body or mind of those whose close application to the business pursuits of life renders an occasional holiday necessary, or the fanciful imagination of the poet, may rest with a satisfaction that may never be realized in distant lands that are more celebrated in poetry and in song.

Nor must our "magnetic and mineral springs" pass unheeded by. Here the healing and life-giving waters are for ever freely flowing, whose invigorating properties have restored to health thousands of suffering humanity whose complicated diseases have baffled the skill of the world's wisest physicians.

Of the 36,128,640 acres of lands in the State of Michigan, over thirteen and a half millions of acres, or more than one-third the entire area, have been granted to the State for various purposes by the General Government, as will appear from the following statement:

	Acres.
For Primary Schools (estimated),	1,067,000
University,	46,080
Internal Improvement,'	500,000
State Building,	3,200
Salt Spring (Normal School and Asylum),	46,080
Swamp,	5,836,900
Agricultural College,	235,673
Ship Canals,	1,250,000
Wagon Roads,	1,718,613
Railroad purposes,	2,909,103
Total,	13,612,649

There are yet vacant and subject to sale lands estimated as follows: swamp, 2,250,000 acres; primary school, 400,000 acres; agricultural college, 188,000 acres. And it may be of interest here to remark that the swamp lands are not in all cases what the term swamp literally signifies, but that many of them are susceptible of being converted into the most productive farms for grass, grain, and fruit-growing purposes, and that the State offers them *free to all* who will comply with the terms of the law, and without the payment of a dollar in money. The primary school lands consist of section numbered sixteen in each township (soon to be augmented by the addition of 49,000 acres selected from the best Government lands), and these are held for sale at four dollars per acre, cash, if valuable principally for timber, or, if the chief value is for agricultural purposes, three-fourths of the purchase price may remain on interest at seven per cent., thus giving easy terms to all who wish to secure and improve homes.

The agricultural college lands were selected with special reference to their value for farming purposes, and such are held for sale at three dollars per acre, on the same terms of payment as the school lands. There are some choice pine and other timber lands in this selection, and these are held at five dollars per acre, *all cash* at date of purchase. By reference to table No. 21, it will be observed that the sales of primary school and agricultural college lands very much exceed the sales of the same class of lands in any previous year, while the sales of swamp lands fall short of those of the year preceding by twenty-five thousand acres; and grouping these facts with the fact that a much larger amount of money was received on account of sales of swamp lands than ever before, we see an unmistakable indication that the *finances* of the country are in a healthy condition, and that our own State of Michigan is receiving a fair share of the attention of capitalists and others who are seeking permanent homes. Our millions of acres of yet uncultivated land offer the best inducements to the husbandman to come and possess. Our untold mineral wealth says to the capitalist and manufacturer, Here you may erect your workshops, where thousands of cunning artisans may earn a livelihood and a competence for life.

Our primeval forests, our magnificent rivers, our bright and shining lakes, our springing brooks, our wild and picturesque scenery, all invite the philosopher, the poet, the statesman, the divine, to come and gaze, and wonder, and admire, and embrace.

Respectfully submitted.

CHAS. A. EDMONDS,
Commissioner State Land Office.

The Diocese of Detroit, and that of Marquette, comprise this whole State.

The DIOCESE OF DETROIT, established in 1832, comprises the lower peninsula of the State of Michigan. It has (1873) one bishop, living in Detroit; ninety-two priests; and one hundred and forty-seven churches. Catholic population, at least 150,000.

The Diocese of Marquette and Saut-Sainte Marie, established in 1853, comprises the northern peninsula of the State of Michigan. It has (1873) one bishop, residing at Marquette; fifteen priests, and forty churches and stations. Catholic population (in which there are many Indians) not given.

CHAPTER VII.

ILLINOIS, MISSOURI, IOWA, WISCONSIN, AND MINNESOTA.

ILLINOIS

LIES west of Indiana, and has the Mississippi River for its western boundary. This State was, like Indiana, first settled by the French. It was received into the Union in December, 1818. Area, 55,400 square miles. Population in 1870, 2,540,-000, being the fourth State in the Union as regards population; in 1860, 1,387,000. Natives of Ireland in 1870, 120,162; of Germany, 203,758.

In fertility of soil, Illinois is not surpassed by any State in the Union; indeed, it is scarcely equalled. The climate, except in the low river bottoms, and in parts of Southern Illinois, is very good. From the fact, however, that nearly the whole State is one elevated prairie, the changes of the weather are very sudden, and the cold of winter and the heat of summer more intense than in some other States of the same latitude. Land is, in general, dear, ranging from ten to two hundred dollars an acre. Not much land is to be had at the first-named price. In that part of the State lying near the great city of Chicago, there is a growing disposition to sell land in farms of forty, sixty, and eighty acres to gardeners and dairymen. Generally, land is not sold in such small quantities. There is a brisk demand for all kinds of labor; and the price paid for it is as good as it is anywhere, except in the Pacific States.

The following letter is from the Right Rev. Bishop Baltes, of Alton, whose diocese comprises Southern Illinois:

ALTON, February 12, 1873.

REV. S. BYRNE:

DEAR SIR: Though I would very much like to see many good Catholic families make their way from other parts to Illinois, I feel convinced that the chances for the poorer classes are not the most inviting. The land here, as is well known, is rich; markets good, etc.

The land has been taken up by good farmers, and what they have not is in the hands of speculators; consequently, too high-priced for any but those who are pretty well off. Wages for all kinds of work very good.

I am, rev. dear sir, yours,

✠ P. J. BALTES.

It is a fact well known that there is hardly a State in the Union in which Irish people are in so prosperous a condition as in this. It is easily accounted for by the fact that large numbers of them purchased land several years ago from the railroad companies for a low price and on a long credit. The same may be done in other parts of the country now.

There are two Catholic dioceses in Illinois, under the respective titles of Chicago and Alton.

The DIOCESE OF CHICAGO, established in 1824, comprises the northern part of the State, and has one bishop, residing in Chicago; one hundred and sixty-five priests, and twenty-four clerical students; two hundred and twenty-five churches, and a great number of stations; a large number of religious institutions of all kinds. Catholic population not given, but probably amounts to 250,000.

The DIOCESE OF ALTON, established in 1857, comprises Southern Illinois, and has one bishop, residing at Alton; one hundred and six priests, and thirty clerical students; one hundred and forty-two churches, and several stations. Catholic population, 100,000.

MISSOURI

lies west of Illinois, being separated from it by the Mississippi River. This State was first settled by the French, and was admitted into the Union in August, 1821. Area, 67,380 square miles, being twice as large as Ireland. Population in 1870, 1,721,295; in 1860, 1,182,000. Natives of Ireland in 1870, 55,000; of Germany, 114,000. In population, it ranks fifth among the States, coming next after Illinois. The great increase of population in these two States is worthy of note.

Land may be bought in all parts of this flourishing State on very moderate terms. Improved land is held at from seven to thirty or forty dollars an acre, according to the value of improvements, distance to market, etc.; unimproved land may be had at from one to ten dollars an acre generally through the State. Labor of all kinds is in demand, but more especially farm labor.

The city of St. Louis, founded by the French in 1764, is in population and wealth the greatest city of the West.

Catholic Statistics for 1873.

The ARCHDIOCESE OF ST. LOUIS, established in 1826, comprises the southeastern part of the State, and has one archbishop and one coadjutor-bishop, residing at St. Louis; two hundred and ten priests, and forty-eight clerical students; one hundred and sixty-seven churches built, and fourteen building; thirty chapels and stations. There is also a full supply, especially in St. Louis, of religious institutions of all kinds. Catholic population, 170,000

The DIOCESE OF ST. JOSEPH, established in 1868, comprises the northwestern part of the State. It has one bishop, residing at St. Joseph; fourteen priests, and about thirty churches and stations.

Attention is called to the following advertisement relating to land in Southwestern Missouri:

"The Atlantic and Pacific Railroad Company offers 1,200,000 acres of land in Central and Southwest Missouri, at from $3 to $12 per acre, on seven years' time, with free transportation from St. Louis to all purchasers. Climate, soil, timber, mineral wealth, schools, churches, and law-abiding society, invite emigrants from all points to this land of fruits and flowers. For particulars, address A. Tuck, Land Commissioner, St. Louis, Mo."

IOWA

lies directly north of Missouri, and west of the Mississippi River. It became a State in March, 1845. Area,

55,045 square miles. Population in 1870, 1,192,000; in 1860, 675,000. Natives of Ireland in 1870, 40,124; of Germany, 66,162.

The prospects for immigrants in the State of Iowa are not now quite so encouraging as they were a few years ago. But it is a new State, having much undeveloped land, and there are many good chances for the industrious poor even yet. There is very little Government land any more, and what remains is principally in the northwestern part of the State. There are large tracts of railroad lands, however, and this may be purchased on the most favorable terms (from $3 to $12 an acre) and on a long credit, sometimes as long as ten years. The climate and soil are known to be excellent, and, taken all in all, Iowa is one of the best States in the Union. The "Iowa Railroad Land Company" have 1,700,000 acres of good land for sale in this State, and 180,000 acres in Eastern Nebraska. Their Iowa lands range from $3 to $7 an acre, on a three years' credit; they come to more, of course, on a longer credit. Full particulars may be obtained by application in person or by letter to the "Land Commissioner of the Iowa Railroad Land Company, Cedar Rapids, Iowa."

An excellent pamphlet has been published under the supervision of the Iowa Board of Immigration, entitled *Iowa the Home for Immigrants*. It may be obtained, by letter or otherwise, by application to the Secretary of the Iowa Board of Immigration.

The Catholic DIOCESE OF DUBUQUE, established in

1837, comprises the whole State of Iowa, and has (1873) one bishop, living at Dubuque; one hundred and twenty-two priests, and sixty clerical students. Catholic population, about 175,000.

Probably there is no diocese in the United States in which such efforts have been made as in this to encourage and assist the settlement of Irish Catholics. The first bishop, Right Rev. Bishop Loras, gave his best energies to this grand object, and many of his priests followed the example. Hence the fact that there are many wealthy Irish settlements in this State.

WISCONSIN

lies north of Illinois, and west of the State of Michigan and lake of the same name. It was first discovered and settled by the French. It became a State in May, 1848. Area, 54,000 square miles. Population in 1870, 1,054,670; in 1860, 776,000. Natives of Ireland in 1870, 48,500; of Germany, 162,500.

Wisconsin is a rich and well-settled State. The severity of the winter, both here and in Minnesota, constitutes an obstacle to a more rapid settlement of these two States. This obstacle is outbalanced, however, by the great salubrity of the climate and the extraordinary productiveness of the soil. There is little, if any, Government land in this State. Improved land is generally from twenty to one hundred dollars an acre; unimproved, from one to twenty dollars, according to location, nearness to market, and other circumstances. Mechanics of all kinds find plenty of work, especially in Milwaukee and in the other principal towns. Farm and railroad labor is in demand.

There are three Catholic dioceses in this State, namely, those of Milwaukee, La Crosse, and Green Bay.

The Diocese of Milwaukee, established in 1844, comprises the southern part of the State, and has one bishop, living at Milwaukee; one hundred and eighty-six priests, and several clerical students; two hundred and forty-four churches, seventeen chapels, and thirty stations. Catholic population, about 160,000.

The Diocese of La Crosse, established in 1868, comprises the northwestern part of the State, and has one bishop, residing at La Crosse; thirty-four priests, and nine clerical students; seventy churches, and twenty-four stations. Catholic population, about 30,000.

The Diocese of Green Bay, established in 1868, comprises the northeastern part of the State, and has one bishop, residing in Green Bay; forty-eight priests, and twelve clerical students. Catholic population, from 50,000 to 60,000.

The total Catholic population of the State is, therefore, about 250,000.

MINNESOTA

lies north of Iowa and west of Wisconsin. It was first discovered in 1680 by the renowned Franciscan friar, Father Louis Hennepin. It became a State in May, 1858. Population in 1870, 439,706; in 1860, 172,073. Natives of Ireland in 1870, 22,000; of Germany, 41,500.

Area, 83,431 square miles. It is two and a half times as large as Ireland.

It is highly probable that the opportunities of poor men for acquiring homes are better in this State than in any other mentioned in this chapter. The writer acknowledges his gratitude to the Right Rev. Bishop Grace, to the Rev. Father Ireland, and to Mr. Dillon O'Brian, of this State, for information of a very practical character.

The following extracts are from a pamphlet published in 1872, under the supervision of the State Board of Immigration, by the Commissioner of Statistics of the State. The pamphlet is entitled *Minnesota, its Resources and Progress, etc.*, and may be had free by application to the Secretary of State, St. Paul, Minn.

PUBLIC LANDS—HOW AND WHERE TO GET THEM.

According to the latest surveys and estimates, the total area of Minnesota is 51,701,760 acres.

Of this total there are in the hands of private owners about..12,000,000
Held by railroads, schools, etc., about......................13,000,000.

—being a total absorption of 25,000,000 acres of the public lands, and leaving an area of nearly 27,000,000 acres—more than half of the entire State—for the landless and poor of all nations of the earth to enter in and possess. Here is a domain abounding in all the elements of health, beauty, and fertility—an area nearly as large as all the New England States, larger than many of the principalities of Europe, which awaits the developing hand of the frugal and industrious among all classes and conditions of men.

FREE FARMS IN MINNESOTA.

Under the provisions of the homestead law, every settler

who is the head of a family, and a citizen or intended citizen of the United States, may become the owner of a farm of 160 acres without paying for it, by simply cultivating and residing upon the land for five years, and paying the fees of the land officers. And this land, thus acquired without cost, is exempt by law from liability for all debts previously contracted.

This privilege of obtaining free farms under the homestead law is shared by women, whether widows or unmarried ladies, equally with men. The vast region thus open to free settlement comprises every variety of prairie and timber land, and tracts having both, and much of it is rich in minerals and supplies of pine lumber. In some places, smooth, level prairie and heavy timber abruptly come together; in others, the land is covered with a growth of bushes and small trees, with frequent groves and oak openings and belts of timber. In nearly every locality, numerous lakes and streams water and beautify the country, while the soil is a quick, dark loam, which will yield every product known in the temperate zone.

Here every man may enjoy the reward of his labor, and become an independent land proprietor. However poor, he possesses equal rights and equal political opportunities with the rich and prosperous. He is governed by those whom he may choose to elect, and he may himself, if capable and persevering, become the highest officer in the land. Minnesota invites the honest and industrious, however poor and friendless, to make themselves free homes in a country thus blessed with equal laws, a healthy climate, and a fertile soil. The manner in which this may be done is pointed out as follows:

LAND OFFICES.

For the convenience of all who may wish public lands, seven Government land districts have been established in the State, in each of which is a land office. In each of these are two officers, called register and receiver, who conduct the business. The place of location of these offices, and the names of the officers, are as follows:

1. For a district thirty miles wide, and extending from east to west through the State, along the south line. Office at Jackson, in Jackson County. Register, E. P. Freeman; Receiver, J. B. Wakefield.

Good Government land is still to be found in the counties of Jackson, Nobles, Rock, and parts of Pipestone, Murray, and Cottonwood.

2. For a district sixty miles wide, extending east and west, immediately north of the last named. Office at New Ulm, in Brown County. Register, Abner Tibbetts; Receiver, J. C. Rudolph.

Good Government lands yet in the counties of Brown, Redwood, Lyon, Yellow Medicine, and parts of Pipestone, Murray, Cottonwood, and Watonwan.

3. For a district thirty miles wide, north of the above, extending east to the Mississippi River. Office at Litchfield, in Meeker County. Register, J. M. Waldron; Receiver, J. C. Braden.

Good Government land yet in the counties of Lac qui Parle, Chippewa, and parts of Swift and Kandiyohi.

4. For a district twenty-four miles wide, extending eastward from the west line of the State, north of the third, and also extending through the centre of the State northward to the north boundary. Office at St. Cloud. Register, H. L. Gordon; Receiver, T. C. McClure.

Good Government land in Big Stone, Todd, and Wadena, and parts of Kandiyohi, Pope, and Stevens counties.

5. For a district, embracing all townships numbered from 125 to 136 inclusive, from range 35 to the western border, being the counties of Wilkin, Otter Tail, Grant, Douglas, Traverse, and the northern half of Stevens and Pope. Good Government land yet in all these counties, with the possible exception of Douglas. Office at Alexandria, in Douglas County Register, Lars K. Aaker; Receiver, J. H. Vandyke.

6. For a district immediately north of the above, of the same width, and extending to the northern border of the State. Office at Oak Lake, Becker County. Register, W. A. Newton; Receiver, Reuben Reynolds.

This district is new, the register's and receiver's offices being (in April) not even opened yet, and most of its Government lands are yet subject to entry under the homestead and preemption laws. The counties of Becker and Clay, traversed by the Northern Pacific R. R., are in this district, and thousands of miles of fertile prairie and openings belong to it.

7. For a district lying between the St. Cloud district and the St. Croix River. Office at Taylor's Falls, in Chisago County. Register, J. P. Owens; Receiver, Oscar Roos.

8. For the remainder of the State, comprising the territory bounded by Lake Superior, by British America, and by districts 4 and 7. Office at Duluth. Register, Ansell Smith; Receiver, W. H. Feller.

CLASSES OF PUBLIC LANDS.

There are three classes of public lands:

1. All lands outside the limits of the lines of the several land-grant railroads in this State. These are held at $1 25 per acre.

2. All public lands comprising the even-numbered sections within the limits of railroad grants, which are $2 50 per acre.

3. The lands formerly reserved for the Sioux Indians, which, until offered for sale, are subject to pre-emption by actual settlers at their appraised value.

The two first may be had at all the land offices, and the third at the New Ulm and Litchfield offices only.

I have also before me a pamphlet, prepared by the "Irish Emigration Society of St. Paul," on the same subject. The statements of both agree substantially, and hence there is no need of extracts from the last-named pamphlet. It may be obtained *free* by addressing the *Northwestern Chronicle*, St. Paul's, Minn.

The Diocese of St. Paul, established in 1850, comprises the whole State of Minnesota and that part of Dakota lying east of the Missouri River. It has one bishop, residing at St. Paul's; seventy-seven priests, and seventeen clerical students; one hundred and sixty churches, and eighty-four stations. Catholic population, about 125,000.

CHAPTER VIII.

THE STATES OF KANSAS AND NEBRASKA, AND THE TERRITORIES OF DAKOTA, WYOMING, AND MONTANA.

KANSAS

LIES directly west of Missouri and south of Nebraska. It became a State in January, 1861. Area, 81,318 square miles. Population in 1870, 364,399; in 1860, 107,206. Natives of Ireland in 1870, 11,000; of Germany, 12,700.

The extraordinary progress of this State in wealth and population is the most substantial proof of the goodness of the soil and healthfulness of the climate. There is a great deal of Government land not yet taken up; and the railroad lands, offering superior advantages, are very extensive.

I am indebted to the Right Rev. Bishop Fink, of the Benedictine Order, for the following clear, practical, and valuable information regarding the prospects of immigrants in this State. The pains to which he has put himself to give a brief and yet a complete exposition of the subject bespeak the training of the scholar and the charity of the Christian.

LEAVENWORTH, KANSAS, March, 1873.

REV. S. BYRNE, O.S.D.:

REV. FATHER: When I received your letter, requesting me to give you some items regarding immigration into this State, and what would be the prospects for immigrants, I intended answering much sooner; however, official duties and the routine of business have made me put off the reply longer than anticipated. Yourself and kind readers need not expect anything from me but a mere sketch for practical purposes. For the sake of perspicuity, I will divide the letter into several headings.

SOIL.

1. The soil is very productive throughout, mostly presenting a rolling surface, thus affording superior drainage. Every kind of grain and fruit can be grown; it is especially adapted to the growing of the grape. The rich, black soil is generally from two to six feet and more thick.

LANDS FOR SALE.

2. There are millions of acres of the best land for sale by the various railroads alone that run through Kansas; besides these, there are the "homestead lands."

CLIMATE.

3. The climate is very salubrious thoughout; new sections of the country are visited by intermittent fever in spring and fall, which disappears with the progress of the cultivation of the soil. Vast numbers of people, who had been in feeble health in the more eastern States, contend that they have been greatly benefited by our climate; the summer heat is rendered less oppressive and excessive by a continual breeze, and the nights are very refreshing. The winters are compara-

tively short; but Kansas has very cold spells during her winters, and the poor buffalo-hunters have been overtaken unawares by such cold snaps, so that frozen limbs, and even death, have been the consequence. Let those who come have good winter clothing; they will need it, though not as long as in States lying more north than Kansas.

TIMBER—COAL—WATER.

4. Kansas has not a great deal of timber, except in certain sections of the State, owing to the prairie fires; there is generally hardly any timber, except along the rivers and creeks. For building purposes, lumber has to be shipped hither; in some regions, there is enough of wood along the rivers and creeks for fuel and fence-posts. Even cord-wood sells at from five to six dollars. There is plenty of coal all over the State, and several mines have already been opened and worked. Water is plenty everywhere, and generally of excellent quality. Kansas is as well watered by rivers and creeks as any of the best States of the Union.

WHAT LANDS TO SELECT.

5. Unhesitatingly I would advise immigrants to select lands along the different lines of railroads, on account of greater facilities of access; of being nearer to settlements; of being more within reach of the ordinary commodities of life, and of a better market for produce. The railroads generally hold their lands at such low figures that they are by far preferable to out-of-the-way homestead lands.

HOW AND WHERE TO SELECT LAND.

6. The land is of equally good quality almost everywhere. In the south and southwest, the soil is sometimes a little deeper than in the north or northwest; the north sometimes has more woodland; so that, on the whole, I find little or no difference. I give below the offices of the various railroad land departments, with price of land and general terms.

In the *southeast*, there is the Missouri River, Fort Scott, and Gulf Railroad, owning and selling about three hundred and fifty thousand acres in Bourbon, Crawford, and Cherokee Counties, the price ranging from four to twelve dollars per acre; sold on credit, running through ten years, at seven per cent. annual interest; twenty per cent. discount for cash. The land is excellent; plenty of coal in the neigborhood. Several Catholic congregations are already in existence in that neighborhood. For land, address Mr. John A. Clark, Land Commissioner, Fort Scott, Kansas. To find out what facilities for satisfying your spiritual wants before purchasing, address Rev. M. J. Doherty, at Fort Scott, or Rev. E. Bononcini, at Baxter Springs, or Rev. John Schoenmakers, S.J., at Osage Mission, Kansas.

In the southeast is also the Leavenworth, Lawrence, and Galveston Railroad lands. In some portions of this land, the rocky stratum underlying the soil crops out and forms the surface; excepting such portions, the land is of very good quality, ranging at about the same price. Address John W. Scott, Land Commissioner, at Chanute. To find out, before making any purchases, where there is a church or Catholic settlement, address Very Rev. A. Heiman, at Scipio P. O.; for land south of this, you may address Rev. R. Deusterman, at Humboldt.

The *southwest* is traversed by the Atchison, Topeka, and Santa Fé R.R., owning and selling over three millions of acres along its line; price of land ranging from two to eight dollars per acre; time for payment, eleven years, with 7 per cent. interest, besides other very favorable conditions. The land of this company is very superior, though there is scarcity of timber. For information about land, etc., address A. E. Touzalin, Land Commissioner, at Topeka; but before, and for actual location, address Rev. F. Swembergh, at Wichita, Rev. Jos. Perrier, or Rev. J. H. Defouri, both at Topeka, Kansas.

The *west* is traversed by the Kansas Pacific R. R. Along its line from east to west there are more Catholic settlements than on any other road at present; it owns and has for sale about six millions of acres, prices ranging from two to six dollars per acre, sold on five years' credit, with interest at six per cent., in this manner: one-fifth cash at time of purchase; for the next two years, only the interest on the balance, etc. For information about land, address John P. Devereux, Land Commissioner, at Lawrence, Kansas; where to find church and Catholic settlements, address Rev. John Fogarty, at Solomon City, Kansas, and Rev. P. Scholl, at Junction City, Kansas.

The *northwest.*—Two railroads run through the northern portion of the State from east to west, along which there are several Catholic settlements. The St. Joseph and Denver R. R. has about 100,000 acres in Marshall, Washington, Republic, Jewel, Cloud, Ottawa, and Riley Counties, for sale at from three to six dollars, one-fifth of which is payable in cash at time of purchase, the balance in five equal annual payments, with ten per cent. interest. For information about land, address D. M. Steele, President Kansas Land Company, at St. Joseph, Missouri; to find out the location of Catholic settlements, address Rev. A. Weikmann, at Hanover, or Rev. Thos. O'Reiley, at Frankfort, or Rev. L. Mollier, at Concordia, Kansas.

For information about land owned by the Central Branch U. P. R. R., address Major W. F. Downs and the Very Rev. Father Giles Christoph, O.S.B., at Atchison, or Rev. Th. Bartl, at Severance P. O., or Rev. Timothy Luber, at Seneca, Kansas.

WHO OUGHT TO COME TO KANSAS.

In the foregoing, it will be found that my aim has been to assist such as wish to come here to settle on land for farming purposes; that I have hardly mentioned anything about mechanics, nothing about cities; though there are a number of the latter, and thousands of the former, who gain a good livelihood, and form a very respectable and numerous class of our citizens. However, it is farmers I wish to induce to come out here, before the best of this beautiful land is taken up by parties of every description but Catholics. At the same time, I wish it to be understood that immigrants ought to have some means to pay part of purchase money, to fence a few acres of land, to get up a little shanty, to buy a cow, a span of horses, and the most necessary agricultural implements, and to support one's self till the next crop can be harvested; parties that come here with nothing, and settle on the land, will soon find out their mistake, and leave in disgust. A good plan would be to select land, pay as much as is required, and earn at your trade what you can to pay for your land, and have it broken, for which about three dollars per acre is paid; have a crop put in, and the proceeds will almost pay you for your expenses; yourself, in the meantime, working at your trade. What a happy home could thousands of families find by settling on our fine lands!

Immigration has of late years been very great, though the Catholics have not been in due proportion. There are some thirty thousand Catholics in the State, that form about one-sixteenth of the whole population. As it would be very desirable to locate either in Catholic settlements, or to form new ones, people of the same nationality ought to settle together as much as possible; if large tracts of land could be taken up together and at once, it would obviate a good many difficulties otherwise to be encountered; spring is the most desirable time for immigration.

By way of making myself useful to parties that desire to go on homestead land, I wish to state that there is plenty of it yet, but would advise parties to come in large numbers. Norton and adjacent counties contain very fine land, and several good-sized streams pass through; that portion of the country is said to be pretty well timbered. A large portion of the northwest and southwest of Kansas has not even been divided into counties yet; Norton and Graham Counties are the two last of the northwest portion, with hardly any inhabitants, except a few adventurous pioneers. Let there be a great exodus from the overcrowded cities in the East of industrious Irishmen; in a few years they will be well to do, and their children, growing up around them, will bless them.

Very respectfully,

✠ LOUIS M. FINK, O.S.B.,

Coadjutor Bishop.

I am indebted, also, to Hon. R. W. P. Muse for special information regarding the lands of the Atchison, Topeka, and Santa Fé Railroad. These have been already referred to in Bishop Fink's letter. Inasmuch as both accounts agree exactly, I do not deem it necessary to insert any further particulars here. The principal agent, A. E. Touzalin, may always be addressed at Topeka, Kansas, for full information.

Catholic Statistics.

The VICARIATE APOSTOLIC OF KANSAS, established in 1851, has two vicars apostolic, residing at Leavenworth; forty-eight priests, and several clerical students; fifty-five churches built, and sixteen building. There are several religious institutions, both male and female. Catholic population, 30,000.

NEBRASKA

lies north of Kansas, and west of Iowa, having for its eastern boundary the Missouri River. It became a State by act of Congress in February, 1867. Area, 76,000 square miles. Population in 1870, 123,000; in 1860, 29,000. Natives of Ireland in 1870, 5,000; of Germany, 11,000.

The peculiar attractions for emigrants to Nebraska are very similar to those of Kansas. The State is traversed by the great railroad route to California—the Union Pacific Railroad—which is 1,037 miles long, and has a land grant of 12,000,000 acres from the Government of the United States. The country is admirably adapted for grazing, and large fortunes are being realized in that branch of industry every year. One of the pioneers in this successful business is a Catholic—Mr. Edward Creighton, of Omaha—whose letter to Dr. Latham I take the liberty of inserting :

OMAHA, NEB., April 15, 1870.

DEAR SIR: I cheerfully give you for publication the result of my experience in grazing in the country west of the Missouri River.

"My first grazing in that country was the winter of 1859. Since then, for eleven winters, I have grazed more or less stock, including horses, sheep, and cattle, in Colorado, Wyoming, Utah, and Montana. The first seven winters I grazed work-oxen mostly. Large work-cattle winter on the grasses in the valleys and on the plains exceedingly well, and are in good condition for summer work by the first of May. The last four winters I have been raising stock, and have had large herds of cows and calves. The present winter I have wintered about eight thousand head. They have done exceedingly well. We have lost very few through the whole winter, and those lost were very thin when winter commenced.

We have no shelter but the bluffs and hills, and no feed but the wild grasses of the country. We have had three thousand sheep the past winter, and they are in the best of order. Many are being sold daily for mutton. Like the cattle, they require no feed nor shelter. The high, rolling character of the country, and the dry climate, and the short, sweet grasses of the numerous hillsides are extremely favorable to sheep-raising and wool-growing. I have been interested in stock-raising in the States for a number of years, where we had tame grass pastures, and tame grass hay, and fenced fields, and good shelter for the stock, and good American and blooded cattle, and an experienced stock-raiser to attend to them; and after a full trial, I have found that with the disadvantage of the vastly inferior Texas cattle, and no hay, nor grain, nor shelter, nothing but the wild grass, there is three times the profit in grazing on the plains; and I have, as a consequence, determined to transfer my interest in stock-raising in the States to the plains.

There is no prospective limit to the pasturage west of the Missouri River.

All the wool, mutton, beef, and horses that the commerce and population of our great country will require a hundred years hence, when the population is as dense as that of Europe, can be produced in this country, and at half the present prices.

Truly yours,

EDWARD CREIGHTON,

President First National Bank of Omaha.

A pamphlet, entitled *The State of Nebraska*, by J. H. Noteware, State Superintendent of Immigration, Omaha, Neb., and a work by Dr. Latham, entitled

Trans-Missouri Stock-raising, from which the foregoing letter is taken, will throw much light upon the resources of this part of the country. Both works may be obtained by application to the Superintendent of Immigration, Omaha, Nebraska.

Catholic Statistics.

The Vicariate Apostolic of Nebraska, established in 1859, comprises the State of Nebraska and the Territories of Wyoming and Montana, and a part of Dakota. It has one vicar apostolic, living in Omaha; nineteen priests, and three students; twenty churches, and fifty-six stations. Catholic population not given.

THE TERRITORY OF DAKOTA

lies north of Nebraska, and west of Minnesota. It is traversed from northwest to southeast by the Missouri River, which is navigable in the summer season through the whole territory, and even to Fort Benton, four hundred miles beyond. In winter, it is frozen. The area of Dakota is 143,000 square miles. Population in 1870, 14,000; in 1860, 5,000. Natives of Ireland in 1870, 888; of Germany, 563. There are many Indians. It became a Territory in March, 1861, and extended then to the Rocky Mountains.

The greater part of the land of this Territory is still owned by the Government, and presents to actual settlers all the advantages of the homestead law already referred to. In the southeastern part, settlements are increasing very fast, being induced thereto by a good climate and fertile soil. The presence of Indians in other parts of the Territory, and the severity of the winters, retard the growth of white population. It is certainly true, however, that young men with small means, or even without other means than health and industry, may easily succeed in obtaining good farms and homes in Dakota. The rivers of the Territory, and the projected railroads, constitute ample means of transportation, present and prospective.

In Catholic affairs, a part of the Territory belongs to the Diocese of St. Paul, and another part to the Vicariate of Nebraska.

THE TERRITORY OF WYOMING

lies west of Nebraska and Dakota. It was organized as a Territory in 1868. Area, 98,000 square miles. Population in 1870, 9,000. Natives of Ireland in 1870, 1,102; of Germany, 652.

This Territory is peculiarly adapted to sheep and cattle-raising. Its southern part is traversed by the Union Pacific Railroad, and this fact of itself ensures a certain degree of prosperity in a country so sparsely inhabited. The resources of this Territory are quite undeveloped; it is particularly rich in minerals. Gold, silver, lead, copper, coal, and iron are found. The climate is very healthy.

The following is a letter from General L. P. Bradley, United States Army, to Dr. Latham, quoted in his work on *Trans-Missouri Stock-raising:*

FORT D. A. RUSSELL, WYOMING TERRITORY,
April 6, 1870.

DR. LATHAM, *Surgeon Union Pacific Railroad:*

DEAR SIR: I respond very cheerfully to your request for information about the climate, soil, grasses, etc., of the country on the east slope of the mountains from the Big Horn down to the Republican and Smoky Hill, which I prospected or scouted pretty thoroughly in 1867 and 1868. From the Smoky Hill, in about latitude 39° north to latitude 44°, the country is very much like that immediately around the Union Pacific Railroad, with which you and the travelling public are familiar. The character of all this country is rolling prairie, very well watered, and abounding in good grasses to such an extent that the assertion may be safely made that the supply of grazing is unlimited.

All of the streams in this range furnish some timber, and many of the tributaries of the Republican, Powder, Tongue, Big Horn, and other rivers are covered with heavy forests of hard and soft wood. All of the bottom-lands on the streams flowing from the mountains are what would be called East good, reliable farming lands, fit to produce any of the regular crops, except, perhaps, corn. The only danger to the corn crop would be, I suppose, the shortness of the season and the frequency of frosts consequent on the extreme altitude of this section.

North of latitude 44° the country changes materially for the better. It is better watered, having an abundance of pure, clear, mountain streams. The soil is richer, the grasses are heavier and stronger, and the climate very much milder than that for several degrees south. I think the valleys of Tongue River, Little Horn, Big Horn, and the Yellowstone will produce corn, and good corn, too. About the other crops, barley, wheat, potatoes, etc., there is no question. This, I take it, shows about the maximum of soil and climate; for there is no question about the value of a country that embraces hundreds of millions of acres, that will produce good crops of cereals and grasses.

The valley of the Big Horn, five to twenty miles in width, by about one hundred miles in length, I regard as one of the choice spots of the earth. Here the climate, soil, scenery, and natural productions combine to make a country I have not seen excelled anywhere from Georgia to Montana, and equalled only by the favorite countries along the Ohio, the Cumberland, or the Tennessee. The prevailing winds are westerly, bringing the mild airs of the Pacific to these inland slopes, and tempering the winters of latitude 45° and 46° to about the temperature of the mountain country of Kentucky and Tennessee.

The value of this country for grazing may be estimated from the fact that good, fine grasses grow evenly all over the country; that the air is so fine that the grasses cure on the ground without losing any of their nutriment, and that the climate is so mild and genial that stock can range and feed all the winter and keep in excellent condition without artificial shelter or fodder. The fact of grasses curing on the ground is a well-known peculiarity of all the high country on the east slope of the mountains, and in this is found the great value of this immense range for grazing purposes.

The difference between grasses which have to be cut and cured and those which are preserved on the ground is enough to convince the stock-raiser and herder of the value of these immense ranges known as "the Plains." I believe that all the flocks and herds in the world could find ample pasturage on these unoccupied plains and the mountain slopes beyond; and the time is not far distant when the largest herds and flocks in the world will be found right here where the grass grows and ripens untouched from one year's end to the other. I believe there is no place in this section of the country, from latitude 47° down, where cattle and sheep will not winter safely with no feed but what they can pick up, and with only the rudest shelter. In the mountains, or in the valleys of the mountain streams, they would find ample shelter from storms in the frequent cañons and ravines.

The mountain ranges are peculiarly adapted to sheep-raising, the range is unlimited, the grasses are fine, and the air is pure and dry—conditions which ensure healthier stock and better wool than the climate and soil of the low country.

I have said that the climate about Big Horn was very mild ; as an indication of this, I will state that the average temperature in the valley, latitude 45° 30′, was in December, 1867, 32° above ; in January, 1868, 20° above ; in February, 40° above ; and in March, 55° above. In August, 1867, the mercury was as high as 107° above. Coal, iron, and fine building-stone are plentiful in the mountains of the Big Horn ranges. Fine clay and limestone are found in abundance, and the mountains furnish good pine timber in fair quantity. Nature has provided most liberally for the wants of civilization in this favored region, and, when it is opened up to settlement, it will attract a large population, and will prove to be a great producing country.

Very truly yours

L. P. BRADLEY,
Brevet Brigadier-General, U. S. A.

There are Catholic priests at Cheyenne and Laramie City. The Territory is included in the Vicariate of Nebraska.

THE TERRITORY OF MONTANA

lies west of Dakota and north of Wyoming. It was organized as a Territory in May, 1864. Area, 144,000 square miles. Population in 1870, 20,595. Natives of Ireland in 1870, 1,635 ; of Germany, 1,233.

The report from this Territory to the United States

Bureau of Statistics is that there is far more good land unoccupied than occupied. Miners are in good demand at five dollars a day; laborers get fifty dollars a month, with board. Female labor is in great demand at very high wages. The river Missouri rises in this Territory, and is navigable from Fort Benton to Dakota—a distance of four hundred miles.

The reverend fathers of the Society of Jesus have a church at Helena, from which they attend a great number of stations. The Territory is included in the Vicariate of Nebraska. There are fifteen hundred Catholic Indians in charge of these devoted fathers.

CHAPTER IX.

THE TERRITORIES OF NEW MEXICO, ARIZONA, COLORADO, UTAH, AND IDAHO.

NEW MEXICO

LIES west of Texas and south of Colorado. It was constituted a Territory in December, 1850, having been ceded by Mexico after the war of 1847. Area, 122,000 square miles. Population in 1870, 92,000; in 1860 93,516 (it then comprised Arizona). Natives of Ireland in 1870, 543; of Germany, 582.

In the valley of the Rio Grande, agriculture is successfully pursued; but a great part of the soil is sterile. Although very near the torrid zone, the climate is temperate, owing to the great elevation of the country and to the fact that many of the mountains are covered with perpetual snow. Most of the inhabitants are Mexicans of the old Spanish race, and are Catholics.

The DIOCESE OF SANTA FE, established in 1850, comprises the whole Territory of New Mexico, and has one bishop, living in Santa Fé; forty-five priests; twenty-eight churches, and one hundred and sixty-two chapels, regularly attended. There are five convents, two colleges, an orphan asylum, and a hospital. Catholic population, 90,000, of whom eight thousand are Indians, and one thousand Americans.

ARIZONA

lies west of New Mexico and east of Southern California. It was made a Territory in February, 1863. Area, 114,000 square miles. Population in 1870, 9,658. Natives of Ireland in 1870, 500; of Germany, 379.

There are mines of gold and silver, copper and lead, in this State. Millions of acres of land are open to the settler. Being for the most part mountainous, the summers are temperate, and the winters are rarely, if ever, cold. There are many Indians in this Territory.

The VICARIATE APOSTOLIC OF ARIZONA was established in 1869, and comprises the whole Territory of the same name, the Mesilla Valley of New Mexico, and El Paso County in Texas. It has one vicar apostolic, residing in Tucson; eleven priests; with several churches and stations. Catholic population not given.

COLORADO

lies north of New Mexico and west of Kansas. It was organized as a Territory in March, 1861. Area, 140,643 square miles. Population in 1870, 40,000. Natives of Ireland in 1870, 1,685; of Germany, 1,456.

This Territory receives its population principally on account of its mining resources, more especially the gold mines of Pike's Peak. The yield of gold-mining in 1870 was $5,500,000. It is very well adapted, also, for grazing, and agriculture flourishes in some parts. It is a favorite resort of invalids, especially of consumptives. There is every probability that Colorado will, in a few years, become one of the most prosperous States west of the Mississippi, and the advantages of settling there now are apparent to all enterprising and industrious men.

The following is an extract from the report of the Territorial Board of Immigration for 1873:

PUBLIC AND RAILWAY LANDS.

There are large tracts of land in Colorado still belonging to the public domain, and open to entry under the homestead and pre-emption acts of Congress.

Land offices are established at Denver, Central, Fairplay, and Pueblo, and those who desire to avail themselves of the liberal terms held out by the Government can do so with comparatively little trouble and expense.

The Kansas Pacific Railway, starting from the Missouri River at Kansas City, Missouri, and Leavenworth, Kansas, extends westward through the entire length of the latter State, then traverses Colorado for more than two hundred miles to Denver, where it terminates. The Denver Pacific Railway starts from Denver, and runs almost due north one hundred and six miles to Cheyenne, and there forms a junction with the Union Pacific Railroad. Both the roads named received grants of land from the Government of almost thirteen thousand acres per mile, in alternate sections of six hundred and forty acres each, for twenty miles on each side of the road. The quantity of land in the Territory owned by the two roads is about three million of acres, including the very best of farming, grazing, and coal land, and much good timber. It is sold for cash at a reasonable valuation, or on five years' time upon the following plan, the example being for one hundred and sixty acres, sold March 1, 1873, at five dollars per acre:

	Principal.	Interest.	Total.
Cash payment	$160 00	$38 40	$198 40
Due March 1, 1874	....	38 40	38 40
" " " 1875	160 00	28 80	188 80
" " " 1876	160 00	19 20	179 20
" " " 1877	160 00	9 60	169 60
" " " 1878	160 00	....	160 00
			$934 40

No payment of principal is required at the end of the first year, thereby giving the settler a chance to put all his earnings and profits into the improvement of his new home. The railway companies make liberal reduction upon transportation rates from the Missouri River to Colorado, for persons or colonies who become purchasers of railway lands.

Messrs. Byers & Parker, Denver, Colorado, are sole agents for the sale of railway land in the Territory. They send out pamphlets and maps, and will answer all enquiries in regard to railway lands.

The VICARIATE APOSTOLIC OF COLORADO, established in 1868, comprises the Territory of Colorado, and has one vicar apostolic, residing at Denver City; fifteen priests, and four clerical students; seventeen churches and chapels built, and fourteen building; thirty-five stations. Catholic population, 16,000.

UTAH

lies west of Colorado, and became a Territory in September, 1850. It was settled by the Mormons, whose peculiar religious tenet resembles that of the Mahometans, which is polygamy. They make up the principal part of the population at present; but it is supposed that a large immigration of persons of other religious views is now setting in. The area of the Territory is 88,000 square miles. Population in 1870, 87,000; in 1860, 41,000. Natives of Ireland in 1870, 502; of Germany, 358. The other foreign nationalities in Utah are: English, 16,070; Scotch, 2,391; Welsh, 1,783; Danish, 5,000; and Swedes, 1,800.

The climate of this Territory is mild and uniform; the soil is productive in the valleys, but generally sterile elsewhere. It is expected that extensive mining operations will soon be inaugurated. The Central Pacific Railroad from California meets the Union Pacific at Ogden, in this Territory.

There are very few Catholics, and they are visited from Idaho.

IDAHO

lies north of Utah and west of Wyoming and Montana. It became a Territory in March, 1863. Area, 91,000 square miles. Population in 1870, 15,000. Natives of Ireland in 1870, 1,000; of Germany, 600.

There is a vast amount of unoccupied land in this Territory, all of which is subject to entry under the laws of the United States, on the terms already frequently mentioned. There is much mining carried on here; and the mines furnish a ready market for all kinds of produce. The river valleys are extremely fertile, and the other parts of the Territory are adapted for grazing. The chances for the industrious poor are very good here.

The VICARIATE APOSTOLIC OF IDAHO comprises the Territory of Idaho and that part of Montana lying west of the Rocky Mountains. It was established in 1868, and has one vicar apostolic, living in Idaho City; thirteen priests, and twelve churches. There are many Indian missions under the charge of the reverend Jesuit fathers.

CHAPTER X.

THE STATES OF THE PACIFIC COAST — CALIFORNIA, NEVADA, OREGON, AND THE TERRITORY OF WASHINGTON.

CALIFORNIA

LIES along the eastern shore of the Pacific Ocean, having a coast-line of eight hundred miles. It was originally settled by the Spaniards; and was ceded to the United States by treaty with Mexico in 1848. It became a State in September, 1850. Area, 159,000 square miles. It is nearly five times as large as Ireland. Population in 1870, 560,000; in 1860, 380,000. Natives of Ireland in 1870, 54,421; of Germany, 29,701.

California presents unlimited advantages to small capitalists, or to industrious, steady men or women without capital, in climate, richness of soil, variety of productions, and general progress. Although the State was first sought on account of its gold mines, it has been discovered that the great staple products, such as wheat, wool, wine, and even cotton, promise greater profits and more lasting than gold-digging. In the produce of wool, for instance, California is only surpassed by Ohio; and considerably more than one-half of all the wine of the United States is produced here. I have before me a most valuable pamphlet, entitled *All about California* *and the Inducements to settle there*, which may be obtained gratis by application to the California Immigration Union, 316 California Street, San Francisco, Cal. It furnishes, in a brief compass, all necessary information regarding this great State up to 1872. On pages 41–43, it will be seen that good farming lands may be purchased for sums ranging from one dollar and fifty cents to five dollars an acre; and that there are 44,000,000 acres of Government land open to settlement on the "homestead" principle. It is needless to speak of the mines of California, as they are of world-wide celebrity.*

I take great pleasure in giving a place here to the following letters received from most reliable persons in Southern, Central, and Northern California:

We begin with the letter of the Rev. Charles Flanagan, attached to the Church of Our Lady of Angels, Los Angeles. Though brief, it is a valuable document:

LOS ANGELES, CAL., March 4, 1873.

REV. DEAR SIR: The Right Rev. Bishop Amat has given me your letter of enquiry, bearing date January 15, 1873, and has left it optional with me to give categorical answers to each of your questions to the best of my judgment. I do not, by any means, wish to take upon myself the responsibility of encouraging immigrants to come and settle in the county of Los Angeles; I should, however, have no difficulty in doing so, could we hope to be blessed, in every year to come,

* Gold was first discovered by J. W. Marshall, on the farm of General Sutter, about sixty miles east of Sacramento, on the 19th of January, 1848.

with such abundant rains as have, since December last, so favored the agriculturists as to enable them to sow broadcast thousands upon thousands of acres of this rich and virgin soil. In order that you may judge for yourself, I send you copies of the local papers containing a description of the "resources," the prices of land, the amount of wages, and other items, from which, after making the usual allowance for newspaper puffery and exaggeration, you can come to a fair conclusion about the condition of the country. There is one thing about which you may rest assured there is and can be no exaggeration—the superiority of the climate, which cannot be excelled, or perhaps equalled, in the world.

I am, reverend dear sir, with much respect for your zeal, and a prayer for the success of your praiseworthy undertaking, yours faithfully,

CHARLES FLANAGAN.

The following letter is from a most reliable source, and will give a good idea of Central California:

SAN FRANCISCO, CAL., February 18, 1873.

REV. DEAR SIR: Your favor of the 15th ult. has been received. In reply (besides sending works, in which you will find much useful information), I would say that, for salubrity and pleasantness, our climate cannot be surpassed. In the "coldest" season along the seaboard, the thermometer hardly ever goes below fifty-six degrees Fahr. In the interior, and towards the Sierra Nevada Mountains, it sometimes descends to forty degrees Fahr., but never lower. At such a place, we would consider the inhabitants as living in the "cold" regions. There is every variety of soil from the deep loam of the valleys to the light, gravelly soil in the neighborhood of the mountains. Our valleys are amongst the most fertile in the world, and the "rolling" lands of several of our counties are very productive and admirably adapted to grazing and agriculture. Many of our hilly slopes are well adapted to the cultivation of the vine; and those who have made the experiment have succeeded very well in vine culture. In the interior and remote parts of the State, I believe that some good lands may be got yet for the Government price; but not much of this is now open to settlement. In the immediate neighborhood of the large cities and towns, land ranges in price from one hundred to five hundred, and even one thousand, dollars per acre. But at some distance from the principal cities, and not far from promising and rising towns, excellent land may be bought for from ten to thirty dollars an acre. In some cases, this would include a dwelling and the other buildings necessary for a farmer. When speaking of the "coldest" season, I forgot to state that in summer the thermometer ranges from seventy to one hundred degrees Fahr.; but even in the hottest parts of the State, especially towards the higher grounds, where the thermometer is up to ninety-six or one hundred degrees, there is a lightness and freshness of atmosphere, without that sense of suffocation often felt in the State of New York and other Atlantic States, which takes away a great deal from the heat, and makes you feel comfortable. Along the coast, however, the thermometer hardly ever rises above seventy-five degrees, and throughout the summer it generally keeps a little below seventy degrees. In the lower part of the State, farmers are more apt to suffer some odd year from the want of rain than in the northern. But generally other rainy years secure abundant crops in some places; and in many places, very large. I think last year there were over twenty-one million of bushels of wheat raised in the three valleys of Sacramento, San Joaquin, and Livermore."

The two following letters are from Marysville, in Northern California, written by, or at the instance of, the Right Rev. Bishop O'Connell. They refer principally to Northern California, and will be read with great interest:

St. Joseph's Church, Marysville, February 5, 1873.

Rev. and Dear Sir: I am just in receipt of your communication of January the 8th. I highly approve of the object of your work, which I trust will confer a benefit on many thousands. The work, had it appeared ten years sooner, would be of incalculable value; but even now it is not too late. Regarding the prospects in this diocese which with safety can be held out to the poor Catholic emigrant, I would not say that they are what they have hitherto been, but even now they are encouraging. 'Tis true we have many poor Catholic families already; but the greater part of them are so because of a fatal error, viz., they wish to live in every respect on an equality with their more wealthy neighbors. There must be acknowledged here, as in older countries, degrees in the social as well as in the moral order; that is to say, if people are poor, they should try and live according to their means. This would make many happy and comparatively comfortable who are otherwise in misery and in everything but easy circumstances. The wages generally given the farm hands is one dollar a day, or from thirty to forty dollars per month, together with board. In the spring and harvest time, they get, as a general rule, two dollars per day. Most of the productive lands are taken up; still much is left which with care and industry would prove remunerative, whilst many good farms could be bought at from ten to twenty-five dollars per acre. The titles are fast becoming perfect, and the hitherto great drawback, "Government grants," are being settled and rectified. Many of those grants are still in the country, and will, by-and-by, be thrown open to purchasers. On the whole, this diocese would afford remunerative labor to thousands who would content themselves and lead sober and industrious lives. With best wishes,

I remain, truly yours,

✠ E. O'CONNELL,

per J. J. CALLAN, *Pro. Secretary.*

VALUE OF OUR LANDS.

P.S.—(The following is an extract taken from the *Call* newspaper:) "The very richest land in the greatest valley of the State—that of the Sacramento—between

Marysville and Red Bluff, a distance of eighty-three miles by rail, is worth thirty to fifty dollars per acre. Wheat and barley are the favorite crops, and the average yield of each is large. Few cases of failure of crops have ever occurred in any portion of that region, while in many portions of it such a thing as failure from drought is unknown."

MARYSVILLE, February 5, 1873.

REV. DEAR FATHER BYRNE: We have the following agricultural counties: Del Norte, Humboldt, Mendocino, Lake County, Colusi, and a great portion of Yuba, but sparsely inhabited. The most inviting of these counties are Colusi, Humboldt, and Mendocino, which are very productive. An infusion of Irish settlers would be a "God-send," if they could only content themselves with agricultural pursuits.

I remain, yours in Christ,

✠ E. O'CONNELL,
Bishop of Grass Valley.

Catholic Statistics, 1873.

California has the Archdiocese of San Francisco and the Dioceses of Monterey and Los Angeles and Grass Valley.

The ARCHDIOCESE OF SAN FRANCISCO, established in 1853, comprises the central portion of the State and the city of the same name. It has one archbishop, living in San Francisco; one hundred and ten priests, and twenty clerical students; eighty-six churches, and fourteen chapels; a great number of institutions and schools; and a Catholic population of 120,000.

The Diocese of Monterey and Los Angeles, established in 1850, comprises the southern part of California, and has one bishop, residing at Los Angeles; forty-four priests, and three clerical students; thirty churches, nine chapels, and twenty-four stations. Catholic population, 35,000.

The Diocese of Grass Valley, established in 1868, comprises Northern California and Nevada. It has one bishop, living at Marysville; twenty-five priests, and two clerical students; thirty-five churches, and seventy stations. Catholic population, 15,000.

This makes the whole Catholic population of California 170,000—about one-third of the entire population.

NEVADA

lies east of California, and became a State in October, 1864. Area, 112,090 square miles. Population in 1870, 42,500; in 1860, 7,000. Natives of Ireland in 1870, 5,035; of Germany, 2,180.

The principal occupation in this State is mining. The gold and silver mines are very rich and extensive. The western part of the State is generally adapted for farming; the rest is sterile. The Central Pacific Railroad passes through the northern part of the State.

There are about six Catholic clergymen in this State, which belongs to the Diocese of Grass Valley in California.

OREGON

lies north of California and west of Idaho. It has a coast-line of three hundred miles along the Pacific Ocean. It became a State in February, 1859. Area, 95,000 square miles. Population in 1870, 91,000; in 1860, 52,460. Natives of Ireland in 1870, 1,967; of Germany, 1,871.

This State is traversed by three distinct mountain ranges—the Coast Mountains, running near the coast and parallel with it; the Cascades, running parallel with these; and the Blue Mountains, running from the north-eastern part of the State several hundred miles to the California boundary line. The Willamette Valley, one hundred and twenty miles long by about thirty-five miles wide, is between the Coast Mountains and the Cascades. It is by far the most fertile part of the State. West of the Cascade Mountains the rains are excessive, the sun sometimes not appearing for a whole month. Gold has been found in the northern part of the State, and silver, lead, copper, and iron in various places. Fisheries are extensive and lucrative; salmon is caught in nearly all the streams. There is a large amount of unoccupied land which may be had on the Government terms. The demand for labor of all kinds is great. In all of the Pacific States there is a special demand for female labor, or house-help, at wages varying from twenty-five to forty dollars a month. *Oregon as It Is* is the name of a very instructive pamphlet on the resources of this State, by W. L. Adams, a resident of the State for twenty-five years. It may be had for a mere trifle, by application to the *Daily Bulletin* Office, Portland, Oregon. I am indebted to the *Catholic Sentinel* of the same city for many valuable documents.

The ARCHBISHOPRIC OF OREGON CITY, established in 1846, comprises the whole State of Oregon, and has one archbishop, residing at Portland, on the Columbia River; nineteen priests, fifteen churches and chapels. Catholic population, 20,000.

THE TERRITORY OF WASHINGTON

lies directly north of Oregon, and has a coast-line on the Pacific of two hundred and fifty miles. It was organized as a Territory in March, 1853. Area, 70,000 square miles. Population in 1870, 24,000 (probably 30,000 in 1873); in 1860, 11,163. Natives of Ireland in 1870, 1,047; of Germany, 645.

The remarks already made in regard to the resources of Oregon are, as a general rule, applicable to this Territory. Immense quantities of good land may be had on the Government terms, and there is demand for all kinds of labor at good wages. The Northern Pacific Railroad, now running through Northern Minnesota and Montana, is expected to be finished to Puget Sound in this Territory in two or three years. If this is successfully accomplished, it may be expected that Washington Territory will advance most rapidly and soon become a flourishing State.

The following valuable and interesting letter is from the Rev. J. B. Boulet, written at the request of the Most

Rev. Bishop Blanchet, of Vancouver, in the Diocese of Nesqualy:

VANCOUVER, WASHINGTON TERRITORY, Feb. 3, 1873.

REV. SIR: At the request of Right Rev. Bishop Blanchet, I beg leave to submit the following in answer to your favor of the 5th ult.:

LAND.

There are millions of acres of unimproved Government lands open to settlers in this Territory, consisting of natural prairies (best for cultivation), grazing and timber lands. Outside of railroad grants, any one can take a claim of one hundred and sixty acres under the homestead or pre-emption laws. Improved lands are more or less cheap, according to location, improvements, etc., and range from $2 to 10 per acre. Grain is raised in large quantities. Wheat in Eastern Washington averages 25 bushels per acre; oats, 30; corn, 40; rye, 20; potatoes, 300; carrots, 1,000; cabbages, 20,000 lbs.; and hay, 2½ tons. Fruit is also raised in profusion everywhere. In the western section—*i.e.* west of the Cascade Range—wheat averages 30 bushels per acre; oats, 40; and barley, 45. 800 bushels of potatoes, 700 bushels of onions have been raised to the acre, but the average is between 200 and 300 for both. Fruit is also plentiful in this section. Cattle and sheep are extensively raised in the immense grazing lands throughout the Territory for the Oregon, Idaho, and British Columbia markets. This branch of industry pays exceedingly well, as it costs almost nothing to raise them, as they can graze out (with but few exceptions) the whole year round, and command a good price at all times.

COMMERCE.

Lumber is the principal article of export, some two hundred and fifty million feet being manufactured annually, and valued at two and a half million dollars. The exportation of fish, oysters, coal, etc., is yearly increasing and promises well for the future.

POPULATION, CHURCHES, SCHOOLS, RAILROADS, ETC.

The population is estimated at 30,000, of whom 10,000 whites and Indians are Catholics. There are schools in all settlements populous enough to support them. Academies and convents are found in the larger towns. Churches are getting more numerous every year A railroad, the North Pacific, is being built, which in a year or two will connect the principal settlements, and give an impetus to commerce and immigration, and at the terminus of which shall be located a large city, destined to become the great metropolis of the Pacific Coast.

CLIMATE.

In Eastern Washington, the average temperature in spring is fifty-two degrees, in summer seventy-three degrees, in the fall fifty-three degrees, in winter thirty-four degrees. In Western Washington, there are but two seasons—the wet and the dry. The former lasts from November until April, the latter from April till November. Few showers of rain, however, fall during this season. Thunder is almost unknown in this part of the country. The average temperature in winter is thirty-nine degrees, and in summer sixty-three degrees; and what is most remarkable is that even during the hottest days of the summer, the nights are always cool, and a blanket desirable.

WAGES.

Mechanics of all kinds get from three to five dollars gold per day. Good axe-men and teamsters about lumber mills, from sixty to one hundred dollars per month. Laborers in mills, thirty-five to forty dollars. Cooks, from fifty to one hundred dollars, with board. Waiters, from thirty-five to forty dollars, with board. Farm hands, from thirty to forty dollars, with board. Female servants, from twenty-five to forty dollars, with board; the latter especially being in great demand.

In conclusion, I think this country one of the most advantageous for the thousands of families and cotton-mill operatives that are vegetating, and, as you appropriately say, "are lost morally, socially, and physically," in the great centres of the East, and more especially if they have a few savings to start with.

The above extracts were mainly derived from the *Fuget Sound Business Directory;* you may use them in any way that will come within the scope of your proposed work.

Yours most respectfully,

J. B. BOULET.

The Diocese of Nesqualy, established in May 1850, comprises the whole Territory of Washington and has one bishop, residing at Vancouver; fifteen priests, seventeen churches and chapels. Catholic population, 10,000.

TABLE I.

Showing the foreign-born and native population of the several States and Territories on the 1st day of June in the respective years 1870 and 1860.

[From the U. S. Census Report.]

States and Territories.	1870.			1860.		
	Total population.	Native born.	Foreign born.	Total population.	Native born.	Foreign born.
Total U. S....	38,555,983	32,989,437	5,566,546	31,443,321	27,304,624	4,138,697
Total States..	38,113,253	32,640,907	5,472,346	31,183,744	27,084,592	4,099,152
Alabama.......	996,992	987,030	9,962	964,201	951,849	12,352
Arkansas......	484,471	479,445	5,026	435,450	431,850	3,600
California......	560,247	350,416	209,831	379,994	233,466	146,528
Connecticut....	537,454	423,815	113,639	460,147	379,451	80,696
Delaware......	125,015	115,879	9,136	112,216	103,051	9,165
Florida.........	187,748	182,781	4,967	140,424	137,115	3,309
Georgia........	1,184,109	1,172,982	11,127	1,057,286	1,045,615	11,671
Illinois.........	2,539,891	2,024,693	515,198	1,711,951	1,387,308	324,643
Indiana.........	1,680,637	1,539,163	141,474	1,350,428	1,232,144	118,284
Iowa...........	1,191,792	987,735	204,057	674,913	568,836	106,077
Kansas........	364,399	316,007	48,392	107,206	94,515	12,691
Kentucky......	1,321,011	1,257,613	63,398	1,155,684	1,095,885	59,799
Louisiana......	726,915	665,088	61,827	708,002	627,027	80,975
Maine.........	626,915	578,034	48,881	628,279	590,826	37,453
Maryland......	780,894	697,482	83,412	687,049	609,520	77,529
Massachusetts.	1,457,351	1,104,032	353,319	1,231,066	970,960	260,106
Michigan......	1,184,059	916,049	268,010	749,113	600,020	149,093
Minnesota......	439,706	279,009	160,697	172,023	113,295	58,728
Mississippi.....	827,922	816,731	11,191	791,305	782,747	8,558
Missouri......	1,721,295	1,499,028	222,267	1,182,012	1,021,471	160,541
Nebraska......	122,993	92,245	30,748	28,841	22,490	6,351
Nevada.......	42,991	23,690	18,801	6,857	4,793	2,064
N. Hampshire..	318,300	288,689	29,611	326,073	305,135	20,938
New Jersey....	906,096	717,153	188,943	672,035	549,245	122,790
New York.....	4,382,759	3,244,406	1,138,353	3,880,735	2,879,455	1,001,280
North Carolina	1,071,361	1 068,332	3,029	992,622	989,324	3,298
Ohio...........	2,665,260	2,292,767	372,493	2,329,511	2,011,262	328,249
Oregon.........	90,923	79,323	11,600	52,465	47,342	5,123
Pennsylvania..	3,521,791	2,976,530	545,261	2,906,215	2,475,710	430,505
Rhode Island..	217,353	161,957	55,396	174,620	137,225	37,394
South Carolina.	705,606	697,532	8,074	703,708	693,722	9,986
Tennessee......	1,258,520	1,239,204	19,316	1,109,801	1,088,575	21,226
Texas.........	818,579	756,168	62,411	604,215	560,793	43,422
Vermont.......	330,551	283,396	47,155	315,098	282,355	32,743
Virginia.......	1,225,163	1,211,409	13,754	1,219,630	1,201,117	18,513
West Virginia..	442,014	424,923	17,091	376,688	360,143	16,545
Wisconsin......	1,054,670	690,171	364,499	775,881	498,954	276,927
Total Territ's	442,730	348,530	94,200	259,577	220,032	39,545
Arizona........	9,658	3,849	5,809	....	....	....
Colorado.......	39,864	33,265	6,599	34,277	31,611	2,666
Dakota........	14,181	9,366	4,815	4,837	3,063	1,774
Dist. Columbia	131,700	115,446	16,254	75,080	62,596	12,484
Idaho..........	14,999	7,114	7,885	....	....	....
Montana.......	20,595	12,616	7,979	....	....	....
New Mexico...	91,874	86,254	5,620	93,516	86,793	6,723
Utah..........	86,786	56,084	30,702	40,273	27,519	12,754
Washington...	23,955	18,931	5,024	11,594	8,450	3,144
Wyoming.....	9,118	5,605	3,513	....	....	....

TABLE II.—FARM LABOR.

Showing the average daily wages, with and without board, and the average monthly wages, with board, paid for farm and other labor in the several sections of the country in the year 1870.

STATES.*	DAILY WAGES.										MONTHLY WAGES, WITH BOARD.					
	Experienc'd hands in summer.		Experienc'd hands in winter.		Ordinary hands in summer.		Ordinary hands in winter.		Common laborers at other than farm work.		Experienced hands in summer.	Experienced hands in winter.	Ordinary hands in summer.	Ordinary hands in winter.	Common laborers at other than farm work.	Female servants.
	With board.	Without board.	With board.	Without board.	With board.	Without board.	With board.	Without board.	With board.	Without board.						
United States, exclusive of Pacific States and Territories.																
New England	$1 54	2 04	1 09	1 55	1 20	1 63	0 92	1 24	1 25	1 68	26 46	19 85	20 70	16 38	21 41	10 87
Middle States	1 32	1 76	92	1 36	95	1 36	68	1 08	1 06	1 48	21 77	15 32	16 75	12 45	17 86	8 08
Western States	1 37	1 84	97	1 40	1 03	1 45	77	1 15	1 17	1 64	24 07	18 14	18 33	14 48	21 12	9 43
Southern States	86	1 20	69	92	57	94	53	76	88	1 16	16 11	13 35	12 44	10 07	15 32	7 79
General average	1 27	1 71	92	1 31	94	1 35	0 73	1 06	1 09	1 49	22 10	16 79	17 06	13 34	18 92	9 04
Pacific States and Territories																
Pacific States (in gold)	2 06	2 65	1 47	2 00	1 53	2 16	1 25	1 77	1 82	2 48	43 92	34 88	32 93	26 62	34 94	27 99
Territories (in gold)	2 64	3 28	1 63	2 31	2 00	2 67	1 44	2 09	2 38	3 18	50 82	31 10	39 52	25 45	48 50	29 58
General average	2 35	2 97	1 55	2 16	1 77	2 42	1 35	1 93	2 10	2 83	47 37	32 99	36 23	26 04	41 72	29 29

* The New England States above noticed are the following: Maine, New Hampshire, Vermont, Massachusetts, Connecticut, Rhode Island. The Middle States are; Pennsylvania, Maryland, and West Virginia. The Western States are: Ohio, Kentucky, Illinois, Indiana, Michigan, Wisconsin, Minnesota, Iowa, Missouri, Kansas, Nebraska. The Southern States are: Virginia, North Carolina, South Carolina, Georgia, Florida, Alabama, Mississippi, Tennessee, Arkansas, Louisiana, Texas. The Pacific States are: California, Oregon, Nevada.

TABLE III.—Mechanical Labor.

Showing the average daily wages paid in the several sections of the country to persons employed in the under-mentioned trades in the year 1870.

STATES.	Black-smiths.		Brick-layers or masons.		Cabinet-makers.		Carpen-ters.		Coopers		Painters		Plaster-ers.		Shoe-makers.		Stone-cutters.		Tailors.		Tanners		Tin-smiths.		Wheel-wrights.	
	With board.	Without board.	With board.	Without board.	With board.	Without board.	With board.	Without board.	With board.	Without board.	With board.	Without board.	With board.	Without board.	With board.	Without board.	With board.	Without board.	With board.	Without board.	With board.	Without board.	With board.	Without board.	With board.	Without board.
N. E. States......	2 33	2 84	2 93	3 50	2 37	2 88	2 29	2 79	2 40	2 84	2 35	2 87	2 87	3 40	1 90	2 42	2 98	3 51	2 07	2 60	2 22	2 72	2 23	2 77	2 35	2 88
Middle States....	1·95	2 49	2 80	3 33	1 90	2 45	2 08	2 23	1 98	2 50	2 13	2 65	2 57	3 17	1 71	2 22	2 90	3 41	1 80	2 31	1 85	2 35	1 88	2 44	2 03	2 53
Western States..	2 33	2 88	3 10	3 66	2 25	2 75	2 47	2 98	2 17	2 69	2 45	2 96	3 02	3 55	2 05	2 58	2 96	3 50	2 07	2 60	2 23	2 73	2 21	2 73	2 56	3 09
Southern States..	2 23	2 68	2 51	3 09	1 99	2 61	2 26	2 95	1 95	2 57	2 11	2 81	2 53	3 15	1 78	2 41	2 64	3 29	1 80	2 43	1 95	2 59	1 96	2 60	2 18	2 87
Gen. average..	2 21	2 72	2 84	3 40	2 13	2 67	2 28	2 74	2 13	2 65	2 26	2 82	2 75	3 32	1 86	2 41	2 87	3 43	1 94	2 49	2 06	2 60	2 07	2 63	2 28	2 84
Pacific States & Territories.																										
Pacific States....	3 65	4 49	4 36	5 16	3 78	4 54	3 85	4 65	3 61	4 41	3 82	4 66	4 69	5 52	3 21	4 02	4 39	5 24	3 20	3 74	2 96	3 64	3 49	4 31	3 98	4 93
Territories.......	4 28	5 20	5 69	6 15	4 36	5 44	4 34	5 40	3 82	4 19	4 97	6 06	6 43	7 49	4 04	4 96	5 97	6 96	4 46	5 42	3 54	4 29	4 58	5 61	4 70	5 79
Gen. average..	3 64	4 85	5 03	5 66	4 07	4 99	4 10	5 03	3 72	4 30	4 40	5 36	5 56	6 51	3 53	4 49	5 18	6 10	3 83	4 58	3 25	3 97	4 04	4 96	4 34	5 37

TABLE IV.

Showing the total population of fifty principal cities of the United States, in 1870, with the number of Irish, German, and English people in each at the same date.

NAME OF CITY.	TOTAL POPULATION.	IRISH.	GERMANS.	ENGLISH.
1. New York, N. Y	942,292	202,000	151,203	24,408
2. Philadelphia, Pa	674,022	96,698	50,746	22.034
3. Brooklyn, N. Y	376,099	73,985	36,769	18,832
4. St. Louis, Mo	310,864	32,239	59,040	5.366
5. Chicago, Ill	298,977	40,000	52,316	10,026
6. Baltimore, Md	267,354	15.223	35,276	2,138
7. Boston, Mass	250,526	56.900	5,606	6,000
8. Cincinnati, Ohio	216,239	18,624	49,446	3.524
9. New Orleans, La	191,418	14,693	15,224	2,005
10. San Francisco, Cal	149,473	25,864	13,602	5,166
11. Buffalo, N. Y	117,714	11,264	22,249	3,558
12. Washington, D. C	109,200	6,948	4,131	1,231
13. Newark, N. J	105,059	12,481	15,873	4,040
14. Louisville, Ky	100,753	7,626	14.380	930
15. Cleveland, Ohio	92,829	9.964	15,855	4.530
16. Pittsburg, Pa	86,076	13,119	8,703	2,838
17. Jersey City, N. J	82,546	17,665	7,151	4,005
18. Detroit, Mich	79,577	6,970	12,647	3,282
19. Milwaukee, Wis	71,440	3,784	22,600	1,395
20. Albany, N. Y	69,422	13,276	5,168	1,572
21. Providence, R. I	68,904	12,085	596	2,426
22. Rochester, N. Y	62,386	6,078	7,730	2,530
23. Alleghany, Pa	53,180	4,034	7.665	1,112
24. Richmond, Va	51,038	1,239	1,621	289
25. New Haven, Conn	50,840	9,601	2,423	1,087
26. Charleston, S. C	48,956	2,180	1.826	234
27. Indianapolis, Ind	48,244	3,321	5,286	697
28. Troy, N. Y	46,465	10,877	1.174	1,575
29. Syracuse, N. Y	43,051	5,172	5,062	1,345
30. Worcester, Mass	41,105	8,389	325	893
31. Lowell, Mass	40,928	9,103	34	1,697
32. Memphis, Tenn	40,226	2.987	1,768	589
33. Cambridge, Mass	39,634	7,180	482	1,043
34. Hartford, Conn	37,180	7,438	1,458	787
35. Scranton, Pa	35,092	6,491	3 056	1,444
36. Reading, Pa	33 930	547	2,648	305
37. Paterson, N. J.	33,600	5,124	1,429	3,347
38. Kansas City, Mo	32,260	2,869	1,884	709
39. Mobile, Ala	32,034	2,000	843	386
40. Toledo, Ohio	31,584	3,032	5,341	694
41. Portland, Me	31,413	3,900	82	557
42. Columbus, Ohio	31,274	1,845	3,982	504
43. Wilmington, Del	30,841	3.503	684	613
44. Dayton, Ohio	30,473	1,326	4,962	394
45. Lawrence, Mass	28,921	7.457	467	2.456
46. Utica, N. Y	28,804	3.496	2,822	1,352
47. Charlestown, Mass	28,323	4,803	216	488
48. Savannah, Ga	28,235	2,197	787	251
49. Lynn, Mass	28,233	3,232	17	330
50. Fall River, Mass	26,766	5,572	37	4,042

TABLE V.

Showing the population in 1870 *of the capitals of States, and principal cities and towns that contain upwards of* 8,000 *inhabitants.*

MAINE.

Augusta	7,808
Portland	31.413
Bangor	18,289
Lewiston	13.600
Biddeford	10,282

NEW HAMPSHIRE.

Concord	12,241
Manchester	23,536
Nashua	10,543
Dover	9,294
Portsmouth	9,211

VERMONT.

Montpelier	3,023
Burlington	14,387
Rutland	9,834

MASSACHUSETTS.

Boston	250,526
Worcester	41,105
Lowell	40.928
Cambridge	39,634
Lawrence	28,921
Charlestown	28,323
Lynn	28,233
Fall River	26.766
Springfield	26,703
Salem	24,117
New Bedford	21,320
Taunton	18,629
Chelsea	18 547
Gloucester	15,389
Somerville	14,685
Haverhill	13.092
Newton	12,825
Newburyport	12,595
Adams	12,090
Fitchburg	11,260
Pittsfield	11,112
Holyoke	10,733
Northampton	10,160
Milford	9,890
Chicopee	9,607
Abington	9,308
Waltham	9,065
Weymouth	9,010
West Roxbury	8,683
Woburn	8,560
Marlborough	8,474
N. Bridgewater	8,007

RHODE ISLAND.

Providence	68,904
Newport	12,521
N. Providence	20,495
Woonsocket	11,527
Warwick	10,453

CONNECTICUT.

New Haven	50,840
Hartford	37,180
Bridgeport	18,969
Norwich	16,653
Norwalk	12,119
Middletown	11,126
Waterbury	10,826
Meriden	10.495
Stamford	9,714
New London	9,576
New Britain	9,480
Danbury	8 753
Derby	8,020

NEW YORK.

Albany	76,216
New York	942,292
Brooklyn	396,099
Buffalo	117,715
Rochester	62,385
Troy	46,465
Syracuse	43,051
Utica	28,804
Watervliet	22,609
Oswego	20,910
Newtown	20,274
Poughkeepsie	20,080
Morrisania	19,610
Auburn	17,225
Newburg	17,014
Elmira	15,863
Cohoes	15,357
Flushing	14,650
Hempstead	13,999
Yonkers	12,733
Binghamton	12,692
Lockport	12,426
Johnstown	12,273
Fishkill	11,752
Cortland	11,694
Schenectady	11,026
Rome	11,000
Greenburg	10,790
Huntington	10,704
West Troy	10,693
Oyster Bay	10.595
Saugerties	10.455
Brookhaven	10,159
Rondout	10,114
Ithaca	10,107
Ogdensburg	10,076
Lenox	9,816
New Lots	9.800
Castleton	9.504
Wallkill	9,477
Owego	9,442
Deer Park	9,387
West Farms	9,372
Watertown	9,336
Seneca	9,188
Hudson	8.615
Saratoga Spr'gs	8,537
Plattsburg	8.414
Queensbury	8,387
Wawarsing	8,151

NEW JERSEY.

Trenton	22.874
Newark	105,059
Jersey City	82,546
Paterson	33.579
Elizabeth	20,832
Hoboken	20,297
Camden	20,045
N. Brunswick	15,058
Orange	9.348
Hackensack	8,038

PENNSYLVANIA.

Harrisburg	23.104
Philadelphia	674,022
Pittsburg	86,076
Allegheny	53,180
Scranton	35.092
Reading	33,930
Lancaster	20,233
Erie City	19,646
Williamsport	16,030
Allentown	13,884

TABLE V.—*Continued.*

Pottsville	12,384
York	11,003
Easton	10,987
Norristown	10,753
Altoona	10,610
Wilkesbarre	10,174
E. Birmingham	9,488
Chester City	9,485
Mahanoy	9,400
Titusville	8,639
Birmingham	8,603
Danville	8,436

DELAWARE.

Dover	1,906
Wilmington	30,841

MARYLAND.

Annapolis	5,744
Baltimore	267,354
Frederick	8,526
Cumberland	8,056

DISTRICT OF COLUMBIA.

Washington	109,199
Georgetown	11,384

VIRGINIA.

Richmond	51,038
Norfolk	19,229
Petersburg	18,950
Alexandria	13,570
Portsmouth	10,492
Dan River	10,306
Beverly Manor	8,071

WEST VIRGINIA.

Charlestown	3,162
Wheeling	19,280

NORTH CAROLINA.

Raleigh	7,790
Wilmington	13,446

SOUTH CAROLINA.

Columbia	9,298
Charleston	48,955

GEORGIA.

Atlanta	21,789
Savannah	28,235
Augusta	15,389
Macon	10,810

FLORIDA.

Tallahassee	2,023

ALABAMA.

Montgomery	10,588
Mobile	32,034

MISSISSIPPI.

Jackson	4,234
Vicksburg	12,443
Natchez	9,057

LOUISIANA.

N. Orleans	191,418

TEXAS.

Austin	4,428
Galveston	13,818
San Antonio	12,256
Brenham	9,716
Houston	9,382

ARKANSAS.

Little Rock	12,380

TENNESSEE.

Nashville	25,865
Memphis	40,226
Knoxville	8,682

KENTUCKY.

Frankfort	5,396
Louisville	100,753
Covington	24,505
Newport	15,087
Lexington	14,801

OHIO.

Columbus	31,274
Cincinnati	216,239
Cleveland	92,829
Toledo	31,584
Dayton	30,473
Sandusky	13,000
Springfield	12,652
Hamilton	11,081
Portsmouth	10,592
Zanesville	10,011
Akron	10,006
Chillicothe	8,920
Canton	8,660
Steubenville	8,107
Youngstown	8,075
Mansfield	8,026

MICHIGAN.

Lansing	5,241
Detroit	79,577
Grand Rapids	16,507
Jackson	11,447
East Saginaw	11,350
Kalamazoo	9,181
Adrian	8,438

INDIANA.

Indianapolis	48,244
Evansville	21,830
Fort Wayne	17,718
Terre Haute	16,103
New Albany	15,396
Lafayette	13,506
Logansport	12,191
Madison	10,709
Richmond	9,445

ILLINOIS.

Springfield	17,364
Chicago	298,977
Quincy	24,052
Peoria	22,849
Bloomington	14,590
Aurora	11,162
Rockford	11,049
Galesburg	10,158
Jacksonville	9,203
Alton	8,665
Belleville	8,146

WISCONSIN.

Madison	9,176
Milwaukee	71,440

TABLE V.—*Continued.*

Fond du Lac...	12,764
Oshkosh........	12,663
Racine.........	9,880
Janesville......	8,789

IOWA.

Des Moines....	12,035
Davenport.....	20,038
Dubuque......	18,434
Burlington.....	14,930
Keokuk........	12,766
Council Bluff...	10,020

MISSOURI.

Jefferson City..	4,420
St. Louis.......	310,864
Kansas City....	32,260
St. Joseph......	19,565
Hannibal.......	10,125

KANSAS.

Topeka........	5,790
Leavenworth..	17,873
Lawrence......	8,320

MINNESOTA.

St. Paul........	20,030
Minneapolis....	13,066

CALIFORNIA.

Sacramento....	16,283
San Francisco...	149,473
Oakland........	10,500
Stockton........	10,066
San José........	9,089

OREGON.

Salem..........	1,139
Portland.......	8,293

NEVADA.

Carson City....	3,042

NEBRASKA.

Lincoln........	2,441
Omaha.........	16,083

ARIZONA.

Tucson........	3,224

COLORADO.

Denver........	4,759

DAKOTA.

Yankton........	737

IDAHO.

Boisée City....	995

MONTANA.

Virginia City..	867

NEW MEXICO.

Santa Fé.......	4,765

UTAH.

Salt Lake City..	12,854

WASHINGTON.

Olympia........	1,203

WYOMING.

Cheyenne......	1,450

ALPHABETICAL LIST OF BOOKS

PUBLISHED BY

The Catholic Publication Society,

No. 9 WARREN STREET,

New York.

A Sister's Story,	$2 50
Abridgment of the Christian Doctrine,	30
An Epistle of Jesus Christ,	1 00
An Essay in Aid of a Grammar of Assent,	2 50
An Illustrated History of Ireland,	5 00
An Amicable Discussion,	2 00
Anima Divota,	60
Anne Sévérin,	1 50
Apologia Pro Vita Sua,	2 00
Aspirations of Nature,	1 50
Bibliographia Catholica Americana. To subscribers only,	3 00
Bona Mors,	25
Book of Irish Martyrs,	2 50
Catholic Tracts. 1 vol. 12mo,	1 25
Catholic Hymns and Canticles,	1 00
Catholic Christian Instructed,	50
Catechism of the Council of Trent,	2 00
Christ and the Church,	1 50
Christine,	2 00
Compendious Abstract of the History of Church of Christ,	1 25
Confidence in the Mercy of God	50
Constance Sherwood,	2 00
Cradle Lands,	2 00
Defence of Catholic Principles,	60
Diary of a Sister of Mercy,	1 50
Dion and the Sibyls,	1 50
Dr. Newman's Answer,	75
Early History of the Catholic Church in the Island of New York,	1 50
Elia; or, Spain Fifty Years Ago	1 50
Exposition of the Doctrine of the Catholic Church,	60
—— The same. 32mo,	25
Father Rowland,	60
Familiar Discourses to the Young,	$0 75
Familiar Instructions on Mental Prayer,	75
Genevieve,	60
Glimpses of Pleasant Homes,	1 50
Gropings After Truth,	75
Grounds of Catholic Doctrine,	20
Guide to Catholic Young Women,	1 00
History of the Church, Pise,	7 50
History of England,	1 25
History of the Old and New Testaments,	1 00
Home of the Lost Child,	60
Homilies on the Book of Tobias,	1 00
Hornihold on the Commandments, etc.,	2 00
Hours of the Passion,	60
Hymns and Songs,	40
Illustrated Catholic Family Almanac,	25
Impressions of Spain,	2 00
Imitation of the Blessed Virgin,	60
Interior Christian,	60
In Heaven we Know Our Own,	60
Introduction to a Devout Life,	75
Irish Odes. De Vere,	2 00
Journal of Eugénie de Guérin,	2 00
Lenten Monitor,	60
Letter to a Protestant Friend,	60
Letters to a Prebendary,	75
Letters of Eugénie de Guérin,	2 00
Life of Blessed Margaret Mary,	2 50
Life of St. Vincent de Paul,	45
Life and Letters of Madame Swetchine,	2 00
Life of Mother Margaret Mary Hallahan,	4 00
—— The same. Abridged,	1 25
Life of Father Baker,	2 50

www.ingramcontent.com/pod-product-compliance
Lightning Source LLC
LaVergne TN
LVHW021358110826
845150LV00007B/1700

* 9 7 8 1 4 2 5 5 1 3 0 6 1 *